# Headstarts

One hundred
original
pre-text
activities

Natalie Hess

Longman

**Longman Group UK Limited,**
*Longman House, Burnt Mill, Harlow,*
*Essex CM20 2JE, England*
*and Associated Companies throughout the world.*



This book is produced in association with Pilgrims Language Courses Limited of Canterbury, England.



First published 1991

Set in 10/12 ITC Cheltenham Book

Produced by Longman Singapore Publishers (Pte) Ltd

Printed in Singapore

**British Library Cataloguing in Publication Data**
Hess, Natalie
Headstarts: one hundred original pre-text activities.
(Pilgrims Longman resource books).
1. Non-English speaking students. Curriculum subjects:
I. Title II. Series
428.2407

ISBN 0582 064929

**Acknowledgements**
We are grateful to Random Century Group on behalf of the Estate of Robert Frost & Henry Holt & Co, Inc for permission to include the poem 'The Road Not Taken' by Robert Frost in *The Poetry of Robert Frost* edited by Edward Connery Lathem (pub Jonathan Cape Ltd/ Henry Holt & Co, Inc), US copyright 1916, (c) 1969 by Holt, Rinehart & Winston, Inc. Copyright 1944 by Robert Frost.

**Illustrations**
Cover illustrated by Mark McConnell

## A letter from the Series Editors

Dear Teacher,

This series of teachers' resource books has developed from Pilgrims' involvement in running courses for learners of English and for teachers and teacher trainers.

Our aim is to pass on ideas, techniques and practical activities which we know work in the classroom. Our authors, both Pilgrims teachers and like-minded colleagues in other organisations, present accounts of innovative procedures which will broaden the range of options available to teachers working within communicative and humanistic approaches.

We would be very interested to receive your impressions of the series. If you notice any omissions that we ought to rectify in future editions, or if you think of any interesting variations, please let us know. We will be glad to acknowledge all contributions that we are able to use.

*Seth Lindstromberg*
Series Editor

*Mario Rinvolucri*
Series Consultant

Pilgrims Language Courses
Canterbury
Kent
CT1 3HG
England

## Natalie Hess

Natalie Hess attended Harvard University in the USA where she was awarded a Masters degree in Education.

Throughout her varied career in language teaching, Natalie has taught EFL, ESL and trained language teachers in the USA, Britain, Australia and Israel. She has led teacher training workshops at Pilgrims in Canterbury, Britain and at the Centre of Staff Development at the Hebrew University, Israel. She spent four years as the head of the English department of the Hebrew Gymnasia in Jerusalem and was an executive committee member of ETAI (English Teachers of Israel).

In addition to her teaching achievements, she has co-authored three widely used textbooks, has written a regular column for Jerusalem Student Post and has published many articles on wide-ranging aspects of language teaching in international ELT journals.

Natalie is currently working both on her PhD in English Literature and as an instructor at the Center of English as a Second Language at the University of Arizona. She is married with three grown-up children.

## Dedication

I dedicate this book to my teacher, Dr Ora Zohar, who showed me what a pleasant place the classroom could be and who helped the better teacher in me to emerge.

Natalie Hess

# Contents

# Index of activities

| | | ACTIVITY | LEVEL | SKILLS |
|---|---|---|---|---|
| **1 JUST A FEW CHOSEN LINES** **Using quotations and lines from the text** | 1.1 | Line finding | Beginner + | Dictation; Skimming and scanning; Predicting; Reading out loud; Making up stories |
| | 1.2 | Treasure hunt | Elementary + | Skimming and scanning; Intra-group cooperation; Inter-group competition |
| | 1.3 | Needle in a haystack | Intermediate + | Skimming; Asking questions |
| | 1.4 | Comparing quotations | Higher intermediate + | Reading; Paraphrasing; Interpreting |
| | 1.5 | Fake quotations | Intermediate + | Vocabulary practice; Use of idioms |
| | 1.6 | Debatable quotation | Intermediate + | Interpretation; Sustained speaking |
| | 1.7 | Placing it | Intermediate + | Dictation; Skimming; Comparing texts; Prediction; Sentence writing |
| | 1.8 | Off the wall | Intermediate + | Asking questions; Dictation; Reading |
| | 1.9 | Writing on the wall | Elementary + | Reading; Predicting |
| | 1.10 | Close the gap | Intermediate + | Predicting; Making outlines; Asking questions |
| **2 PERCEIVE AND PONDER** **Using visuals and visualisations** | 2.1 | The mental video | Intermediate + | Describing; Predicting |
| | 2.2 | Gates | Intermediate + | Predicting; Describing |
| | 2.3 | I'm in the picture | Intermediate + | Speaking; Listening; Describing |
| | 2.4 | Faces | Intermediate + | Describing; Story-telling; Asking questions; Writing |
| | 2.5 | Nature walk | Intermediate + | Listening |
| | 2.6 | The shop window list | Intermediate + | Reading; Fluency practice; Discussion |
| | 2.7 | The surrealistic painting | Intermediate + | Predicting; Asking questions; Making notes |
| | 2.8 | Making connections | Intermediate + | Fluency practice; Predicting; Making notes |
| | 2.9 | Picture a symbol | Intermediate + | Explaining; Fluency practice |
| | 2.10 | Picture a process | Intermediate + | Explaining; Asking questions |
| **3 SEE, SELECT AND SUGGEST** **Utilising common objects** | 3.1 | The surprise package | Elementary + | Asking questions; Predicting |
| | 3.2 | Making choices | Elementary + | Fluency practice; Translation; Predicting |
| | 3.3 | Meaningful object | Intermediate + | Fluency practice; Predicting |
| | 3.4 | Kim's game | Intermediate + | Speaking; Predicting |
| | 3.5 | Both ways | Intermediate + | Speaking; Listening |
| | 3.6 | How much? | Intermediate + | Speaking; Listening; Using the third conditional; Predicting |
| | 3.7 | Appliances | Intermediate + | Explaining; Listening |
| | 3.8 | Lost and found | Intermediate + | Describing; Speaking; Listening; Asking questions |
| | 3.9 | The toy car | Intermediate + | Speaking; Listening |
| | 3.10 | Cigarette packet | Intermediate + | Speaking; Listening |
| **4 WORDS, WORDS AND A BIT MORE THAN WORDS** **Making use of key vocabulary** | 4.1 | This makes me think of that | Intermediate + | Speaking; Guessing and predicting; Asking questions; Using modals |
| | 4.2 | Wholesome scattering | Elementary + | Writing sentences; Predicting |
| | 4.3 | Hot or cold | Intermediate + | Categorising; Predicting |
| | 4.4 | Water, water everywhere | Intermediate + | Categorising; Predicting |

| | | ACTIVITY | LEVEL | SKILLS |
|---|---|---|---|---|
| | 4.5 | Chain reaction | Elementary + | Predicting; Making up sentences |
| | 4.6 | Thoughts and feelings | Intermediate + | Categorising; Dictation |
| | 4.7 | The rainbow | Intermediate + | Categorising; Explaining; Predicting |
| | 4.8 | Words on my way | Intermediate + | Categorising; Explaining; Scanning |
| | 4.9 | Advertising words | Intermediate + | Writing; Predicting |
| | 4.10 | Shout it out | Beginner + | Skimming |
| **5 WRITE IT RIGHT** **Using written activities** | 5.1 | The outraged letter | Advanced | Writing; Discussion; Reading |
| | 5.2 | Upside down outrage | Advanced | Discussion; Writing |
| | 5.3 | Take a stand | Advanced | Writing; Discussion; Dictation |
| | 5.4 | Cryptic dictation | Elementary + | Dictation; Skimming |
| | 5.5 | Mini lecture | Elementary + | Note-taking; Lecturing; Dictation; Asking and answering questions |
| | 5.6 | Branching out | Intermediate + | Writing; Sentence completion; Explaining |
| | 5.7 | The archaeological report | Advanced | Describing; Writing; Discussion |
| | 5.8 | Letter of recommendation | Advanced | Dictation; Discussion; Writing; Comparing texts |
| | 5.9 | Dialogue journal | Intermediate + | Writing; Asking questions |
| | 5.10 | Card game | Intermediate + | Writing; Summarising |
| **6 POETIC PRETEXTS** **Using poems and songs** | 6.1 | The bio-poem | Advanced | Speaking; Reading; Writing; Interpretation |
| | 6.2 | The contrast poem | Advanced | Speaking; Writing; Asking questions |
| | 6.3 | The single image poem | Advanced | Speaking; Writing; Listening |
| | 6.4 | The limerick | Advanced | Speaking; Writing |
| | 6.5 | The acrostic | Elementary + | Reading; Speaking; Writing |
| | 6.6 | On your own | Intermediate + | Reading; Explaining; Asking questions |
| | 6.7 | The haiku | Intermediate + | Writing; Speaking |
| | 6.8 | Pieces in place | Advanced | Listening; Reading |
| | 6.9 | Filling spaces | Elementary + | Vocabulary expansion; Intensive listening |
| | 6.10 | Poetic gateway | Advanced | Reading; Interpreting; Speaking |
| **7 NAMING IS TAMING** **Using names and titles** | 7.1 | It sits where it fits | Intermediate + | Predicting; Brainstorming; Scanning; Reading |
| | 7.2 | Scrambled guessing | Advanced | Predicting; Guessing; Speaking |
| | 7.3 | Call it by name | Intermediate + | Discussion; Headline writing |
| | 7.4 | Best choice | Intermediate + | Discussion; Explaining; Predicting |
| | 7.5 | Links in a chain | Intermediate + | Reading; Summarising; Taking notes; Predicting |
| | 7.6 | Who is who? | Advanced | Discussion; Predicting |

# Introduction

I wrote this introduction after I had finished writing this book and perhaps that is the way you ought to go about this project too. Are you about to start a new story with your junior class? Perhaps you are planning to bring in some newpaper articles for your adult education course? Or were you considering reading a play with your advanced students or starting a simplified novel as extensive reading in your intermediate pre-university course?

If something like this looms at the edge of your plans, you, like me and like most EFL professionals, are a text-orientated teacher. You know that the written word, as put to use by talented writers to express thought, is your friend and helpful companion in the classroom.

That's why I think that before reading any further, you might want to glance through the book to see what it has to offer. Do you want to teach a poem next Thursday? Then how about taking a look at Activity 4.1 *This makes me think of that*. Are you considering a controversial essay or article for this Monday? How about taking a peek at Activity 3.5 *Both ways*. Are you working on some technical articles with your vocational class? If so, please take a look at Activity 3.7 *Appliances*.

Still with me? I'm glad, because there is so much I would like to share with you. Let's start with some basic assumptions. I firmly believe that learning, especially learning a language, should be enjoyable. I believe that the language classroom should be a place where both student and teacher find enrichment, empathy and room for personal growth. I believe that the EFL class should be an unthreatening laboratory for both student and teacher – a place where they can try things out, experiment with ideas, explore aspects of their personality and dare to make mistakes. I believe that the best kind of learning is the kind where learning and language acquisition become part and parcel of our emotional make up. All of us have, of course, experienced this. Why is it, for example, that we can't remember Harry's name to save our lives, but we instantly recall Thomas, because that was also the name of our favourite great uncle?

## WHAT ARE HEADSTARTS?

Headstarts are affective pre-text activities and lesson openings. Their aim is to motivate, challenge, and arouse curiosity.

The written text is a treasury of linguistic usage and we hold the key that can unlock this storehouse for our students. As small children we learned our native language by being read fairy tales at bedtime and by having lullabies sung to us. Colourful pictures and oral previews frequently invited us into our first reading passages. The EFL framework, unfortunately, seems to have forgotten such natural headstarts. The activities in this book intend to remind us of them.

Research has shown that an interesting opening to a lesson or unit of lessons has a significant positive influence on learning. It increases concentration, stimulates curiosity, increases imagination and fosters motivation.

We have all known immigrants of long standing in various countries who have mastered the language of the country where they reside on a basic spoken level. They can buy their groceries, chat with the neighbours and watch television, but since they rarely read in that language, their progress is limited by the closed circle of practical usage. So, in one sense, they always remain linguistic outcasts.

For real language expansion that will permit our students to widen their field of expression and strengthen their linguistic self-confidence, we must encourage them to read.

## WHY THE WRITTEN TEXT?

In spite of the great popularity of the electronic media, we, nevertheless, still live in a world bombarded with written texts. Written texts remain our most frequent teaching tools, and rightly so. The reading of a text is not just a matter of decoding symbols into meaning, but also involves a series of complex skills such as skimming, scanning, summarising, analysing, and comparing what is written on the page with our own knowledge of the world. For language teachers, texts are just pretexts. That is, they are the means of showing the forms of language in operation. True, texts are repositories of vocabulary, syntax and idiom. But texts are also rich funds of ideas for introspection, speculation and discussion. What's more, the written text is portable. It does not need an electric outlet or an extension lead. It will function in spite of electrical failure or disk damage!

The word *text* comes from the same root as *textile*. Writing and weaving are indeed related activities. Threads of thought fabricate linguistic meaning, just as literal threads make cloth. It is our role as language teachers to facilitate learning by helping our pupils feel the 'textuality' – the style, flavour, depth and internal connections of a written passage.

## APPROACHING THE TEXT WITH A SENSE OF ADVENTURE

All the activities in *Headstarts* involve approaching a new text with a certain sense of adventure. In many ways, getting into and grappling with a new text in a foreign language is like arriving in a strange city. We don't really know what awaits us there, what complications, innovations, difficulties or pleasures. Like all travellers we need to glance at a map before we step out. Initially, we need not study it in detail. We will do that later as we walk about the city. But we do want to know where the centre is, or whether a river flows through this new city. Each of the activities in *Headstarts* offers such a brief glance at the text prior to entering it.

Not many of the activities I present here are completely original to me. They have evolved over the years through hints, suggestions and promptings from colleagues and students. I have tried to give credit whenever I remembered when and how I learned a specific activity.

## HOW THIS BOOK WORKS

The methodology of *Headstarts* is straightforward and simple. I have kept in mind how busy most of us are. If you glance through the 'Preparation' section of the activities, you will notice that no preparation will take more than about ten minutes' work and many of the activities require no preparation at all. I have tried to make this the kind of book you can pick up at the last minute on one of those days when you just haven't had time to plan, but you still, of course, want to give an interesting lesson.

The materials, too, are basic. In addition to paper and pens there is an occasional picture or household object.

I have tried to imbue all the activities in *Headstarts* with a sense of playfulness as an aid to thought and stimulus to imagination. I have attempted to approach every text by generating emotional involvement in the students. In fact, taking care to do this with every text you use may pay an additional dividend. Students very soon get the idea and contribute their own suggestions about how things may be introduced in a way that grabs attention and interest. There have been times when I have walked into a well-functioning, properly 'warmed up' group and told them that they were about to read an article 'Tigers in India' or 'Industry in Japan', but that I hadn't yet had time to make up a good introduction to the reading passage and did they have any suggestions? Their offers are often surprisingly creative. I recommend this technique as warmly as any other activity presented in this book.

You can apply Headstart activities to many types of text, such as newspaper articles, essays, prose, poetry and drama. Most of these activities work best with intermediate and advanced classes, but they can be adapted for elementary learners. I have used them in classes of secondary students and at university level with monolingual as well as multilingual classes. I have adapted the activities to work in classes of fifteen as well as in classes of forty.

The activities in each of the ten chapters have been grouped together according to the technique or type of material involved in stimulating interest in the main text to come. There is an index of the types and topics of texts used in the activities. This will enable you to find which activity is most suitable for the text you want to teach.

You will probably want to use some of the activities exactly as I have presented them. Being a creative teacher, however, you will probably want to doctor others a bit, so that they better suit your own class or the materials you happen to have. I would of course, love to hear from you to find out just how and why you have made your changes.

## THE HEADINGS

Alongside each activity you will notice a number of headings, such as 'Time', 'Skills' and 'Materials'. It is useful to look at these before you begin each activity.

### TIME

I have given the length of time each activity takes. This is approximately how long the activity has taken in my classes. As you well know, however, each class has a time-life of its own, so that here, too, you will have to feel your way. Some of the activities may strike you as too long for a pre-textual venture. I can only say that I have found such pre-text probings worthwhile. Affective involvement so effectively stimulates language production that the time taken offers highly profitable linguistic returns. Occasionally we tend to forget that we are teaching language and not covering material. So, although an emotive introduction may keep us from reading that extra article, it may well lead to a great deal more language learning. Remember too that some of the Headstarts can be used to introduce whole units of shorter texts on a particular theme or to introduce a long extensive reading, even a novel or a play.

### SKILLS

This doesn't refer only to the four basics of reading, writing, speaking and listening, but includes such linguistic and macro-linguistic skills as: taking dictation, producing sustained speech, note-taking, paraphrasing, interpreting, using idioms, etc.

### MATERIALS

I have also given details of any extras you may need for the activity. I have assumed all classes have access to the basics, such as pens and paper and a white or blackboard. If the activity demands the use of a picture, or some index cards or perhaps felt pens, these are listed.

## HOW TO USE THIS BOOK

Scan the whole book once. Make notes about the activities which seem particularly useful for the texts you are now using. Keep this book at school – in a handy place – so that you can dip into it when making lesson plans or, more importantly, when you haven't had time to make a lesson plan.

Change and adjust activities to suit your mood, your class, and your personality!

Good luck and many happy Headstarts!

*Natalie Hess*
*Center of English as a Second Language*
*University of Arizona*
*Arizona USA*
*May 1990*

# *General techniques*

Some of the activities in this book rely on the use of special teaching techniques. Some of these you may know, and some will be new to you. Whichever, feel free to adapt any of the following techniques to suit yourself or your students.

## Brainstorming

1 The group sits in a circle. One member is the secretary.
2 A topic is given. Members of the group have about five seconds to think. They may wish to write down an idea or two.
3 Clockwise, the students contribute any idea that struck them when the topic was given. You should stress that these may be *any* kind of idea. They need not be reasonable or polished, simply something that came to mind. The secretary notes down all the ideas. The secretary may be a contributor, or being busy, may choose to pass. There is no discussion of ideas at this time. This is simply the time to contribute. A student who has no idea whatsoever may say, 'pass', and be skipped in this round.
4 When one circle of ideas is completed, a second circle may be attempted. Students who passed the first time may have become sufficiently stimulated by their peers to make a contribution in the second round.
5 After the second round is completed, the secretary may ask if the group wants a third and final round.
6 The secretary reads out the list of ideas and a discussion may begin about which of the ideas is relevant to the issue.

What I have given you here is the classic brainstorming procedure. Of course, you can organise sessions in other ways, such as brainstorming in pairs where students take turns blurting out ideas on a topic and jotting them down.

## Bridge sentence

When moving from one activity to another, I use a sentence that I hope will lead into the next phase of activity and also express a link with what went before. For example, if I want the class to discuss the problems of old age, I show them a picture of what looks like a happy older couple. Then, I encourage them to ask all sorts of questions about this pair. Finally, I want them to consider the difficulties of old age. My bridge sentence might be, 'When I look at this seemingly happy couple many things worry me – do any of you feel the same?' Such a sentence will serve as a bridge from the picture to the discussion I want to develop.

## Eliciting

The dictionary defines the word 'elicit' as to 'draw out or evoke'. When I use the verb elicit, I refer to a distinct teaching policy. That is:

*Don't say anything that a student can say.*

As I see it, the teacher should avoid telling students anything until they have been asked what they know. You need never explain a word, a rule in grammar, a concept or a question without prior elicitation. You can ask, 'What do you know about this? Does anyone know the meaning of ...? What do you know about ...?' You can always add to their explanations later. But this may not be necessary. You may well learn something new yourself. There is nothing which frustrates students more than hearing a teacher expound on something they already know. Don't you recall such incidents from your own student life?

So when I say, 'Elicit or explain', I always mean: first, elicit as much as you can and only then, if you really must, explain!

## Extensive reading

This refers to the reading of longer texts outside class. These texts may be discussed in class on a weekly basis, or simply introduced in class and then read at home. Extensive reading focuses on content, not on details of language. It means that students read more or longer texts and look up only the vocabulary which they need in order to follow the overall meaning. School curricula often place a heavy emphasis on extensive reading from the intermediate level upwards. Many of the Headstarts in this collection are especially suitable as introductions to extensive reading at these levels although, of course, they are adaptable for use at all levels.

# ORGANISING THE CLASS

## Class size

Occasionally, I describe the activities as being more suitable for large, small or medium-sized classes. I envisage small classes as having ten to fifteen students, medium-sized classes fifteen to twenty-five students and large classes twenty-five to fifty. With some creative imagination on your part, most of the activities in this book can be adapted to suit all sizes of class.

## Size of text

Most of the activities can be adapted to texts of any length. However, occasionally I mention that an activity is best suited to a long or a short text. By a short text, I mean a text that is no longer than one page. A medium-sized text is one to three pages long. Anything above three pages, I refer to as a long text.

## To group or not to group?

To create the kind of community climate where students are not afraid of taking language risks, it is crucial that we foster a milieu in which they know and like each other. Nothing helps us to do this better than the habitual use of pair and small group work.

You will soon notice that practically all the activities include a pair work or a group work phase. Small groups work well for several reasons. Reticent students who don't open their mouths in whole-class phases will feel peer pressure to do their bit in a small group. The image of the teacher as error sensor vanishes when one is talking strictly to classmates. Small group or pairwork permits students to thrash out their ideas in a low-pressure setting before they attempt to perform before the whole class. Also, people listen better in small groups. After all, they want to be listened to themselves and so must return the favour. The idea that they are making progress for themselves rather than for the teacher gradually takes root if groupwork and pairwork is regular.

Having said all that, I must admit that group and pairwork is not always easy to manage. Some teachers fear losing control. Many teachers feel that most of their learners, particularly adolescents, will not take groupwork seriously but will look on it as unsupervised wasted time. Teachers of monolingual classes complain that even highly motivated students slip into their native language as soon as the central teacher-controlled class framework disappears. Teachers of large classes find groupwork difficult to organise.

These are all legitimate worries. But, with a bit of patience and practice, you can overcome them. It is true that adolescents need a sense of structure in their work. I organise my adolescent groups into foursomes, which I scramble about once a week. In these groups of four, each member has a task. The 'secretary' records and summarises the discussion. The 'monitor' makes sure people only speak the target language. The 'dictionary' ensures an English dictionary is available and looks up the difficult words. The 'chairperson' runs the discussion and makes sure that no one dominates. It goes without saying that the students who tend to dominate should be made chairpeople. To encourage adherence to these rules, I routinely ask groups to hand in a brief summary of their discussion, signed by each participant.

The worry about losing control quickly vanishes as teachers notice the obvious improvement in language skills and classroom atmosphere. There is, in this case, truly nothing to fear but fear itself. A colleague who, after a career of lecture-type teaching, adopted the group method, reported the horrible sinking fear in her stomach as her normally 'civilized' classroom became a field of noisy beehives. The only way she was able to overcome her anxiety was by joining one of the groups and participating in the discussion. This was so lively and interesting, that my friend soon forgot her fears and has started enjoying herself during group phases.

Another colleague reported that she felt guilty about being so passive while her class was working in groups. It's easy to understand such anxiety. Most of us have adopted the notion of teacher as central classroom performer. Still, all of us really want our students, rather than ourselves, to be central. Groupwork helps us to achieve this aim. There is no need for us to remain passive during the group phase. If we circulate among the groups, wisely dividing our attention, we can learn more about our students and how we can help them the most.

In very large classes, students often sit in pairs. Pairwork is thus no problem. Asking a pair to turn around and face another pair, quickly turns pairwork into groupwork. I have done this even in classes of forty students with desks that were nailed to the floor!

For brief activities in a small or medium-sized class, I have found the group of three to be the most effective size of unit.

In monolingual classes, I finish each group activity by asking how many people managed to speak one hundred per cent English. Only a few hands are raised. I praise these students and ask how many think they spoke eighty per cent English? Seventy per cent? Fifty? Let's all try for one hundred per cent next time, I tell them. With enough persistence there is constant progress. As students relax and learn more about each other, an atmosphere develops in which students genuinely feel, 'I want to learn because it is important to me!' Among the fringe benefits of this, as colleagues have reported, is a decline in cheating on tests!

A small but significant point worth mentioning is that standing over a group that is working may be threatening. Instead, you can either crouch next to a group to listen for a while before you move on or, if you wish to stay longer, pull up a chair and join them.

## Forming groups

Groups can be formed in many ways:

- You can ask students to count off to three and form groups of ones, twos and threes.
- You can assign names of fruits, flowers, colours or household objects to students and ask them to find those of their own kind. For example, if in a group of twenty students, you give each student the name of a fruit – peach, plum, apricot, pear – the pears find each other, the peaches find each other and so on. After a bit of pleasant scrambling, you will have formed four groups and revised the names of four fruits. You can practise any basic vocabulary in this way and form your groups at the same time!
- For pairing, half of the students can each place a personal object on a table while the other students close their eyes. Each of the students who has not contributed anything picks up one of the things from the table and finds its owner. This person is their partner.
- You can hold on to the middle of a bunch of twenty long strings. Students each take hold of an end of one of the strings. When you let go, students will find themselves linked to a partner.

Even in adult groups, especially if you teach a two-hour block, it is important to move students around. Also, the climate of the class improves greatly as each student gets to know the other students better. For this reason, do encourage students to change partners or groups, even during one activity. To allow or encourage students to check and compare learning, it is useful, after groups have finished one stage of a task, to join two groups of three to make a group of six or two pairs into a group of four.

When a group activity is finished, I like the groups to report to the whole class. Such group reporting can be handled in several ways. The secretary of the group may report, or the group may choose a spokesperson. (This is usually the most articulate person in the group.) If you want the less orally articulate students to perform in plenary, invite the groups to choose their 'best quiet-thinker' as spokesperson. If they get stuck for words, other group members can always help out by prompting.

## KEEPING A PICTURE FILE

It is a good idea for all EFL teachers to keep their own picture file. I recommend reading newspapers and magazines with a pair of scissors handy. If and when anything strikes your fancy, cut it out and throw it in a cardboard box that you keep under your bed! At one time or another, you will be visited by small children who will be delighted to mount your pictures on backing paper. You can then file them in your permanent picture file under any useful categories. I use the categories: houses, interiors, people, landscapes, faces, foods, clothing, animals, hairdos, shoes, interesting situations and interesting advertisements. I have used them all at one time or another. (See *Visual Impact* by David A Hill, also in the Pilgrims Longman Resource Books series, for more details on creating a picture file.)

## KEEPING AN IDEAS FILE

I recommend going to lectures and workshops with some index cards and taking notes on these. It is also useful to keep index cards in the back of any interesting book you are reading – remember, some of the best EFL ideas come from non-EFL sources. You can later file these away in an index card file. Go through the file occasionally and throw out anything you don't use, or anything that once seemed exciting but has proved to be useless.

## ROLE PLAYING

Some of the activities here have a role playing phase. This is a pairwork technique in which students take on a role and act it out with their partner who plays the interacting role. Before students act out a role play, ask them to visualise the character they are to enact. It is a good idea to ask all students who will act the same role to sit in groups and together visualise their characters. Ask them to envisage how the person looks, how old they are, how they dress, what their occupation is, etc. The more clearly students 'see' their characters, the more successful the role play will be.

## WHAT ABOUT DICTIONARIES?

I firmly believe in the use of anything that will help students learn. Bilingual dictionaries are helpful. In adult multilingual classes, most students bring their own dictionaries and will use them when they feel the need to do so. In monolingual classes, it is helpful to have at least one bilingual dictionary and one English–English dictionary handy. Of course, there are times – such as during extensive readings, when we want to practise skimming and scanning – when we discourage the use of dictionaries. When this is the case we must simply say, 'Please don't use your dictionaries now. During this reading, we want to see how much we can understand without knowing all the words.'

## WHAT ABOUT TRANSLATION?

Translation is one way to check understanding. Adult students are frequently not happy with their knowledge of a word until they can find the closest equivalent in their own language. If you are a speaker of their language, I see no reason why you should always withhold this information. In classes where the teacher does not speak the mother tongue of the students, fellow students can often provide the right word. Some of the activities here involve the deliberate use of translation.

### Acknowledgements

I first learned about brainstorming and bridge sentences from Dr Ora Zohar at the Staff Development Center at the Hebrew University, Jerusalem. I got the idea of the quiet thinker from Laurel Pollard at the Center of English as a Second Language at the University of Arizona.

CHAPTER 1

# Just a few chosen lines

## *Using quotations and lines from the text*

A line from a text is a hint of meaning – something to speculate about, something which helps us locate ourselves within the text. This is why we read book jackets or flip through books before we begin the 'real reading'. This is why many of us must read the ending by the time we reach mid-text. The knowledge does not spoil our reading, rather it enriches and makes us want to know how and in which way we are to reach that ending. For some readers, knowing the end or knowing a few landmarks is exactly what makes it possible for them to read less hastily – to slow down and notice more detail.

### LINE FINDING

**1.1**

**MATERIALS**
None

**LEVEL**
Beginner +

**SKILLS**
Dictation; Skimming and scanning; Predicting; Reading out loud; Making up stories

**TIME**
10 minutes

**SUGGESTED TEXTS**
Non-fiction texts, longer newspaper articles, essays, short fictional prose

*Line finding* combines dictation with scanning a text and predicting content. Imaginative guessing about the content of what one is about to read stimulates the imagination and encourages a dialogue with the text. I have found that if students guess 'correctly', they experience a certain satisfaction, while those who guess at possibilities not present in the text are amused at their divergence from the writer's thinking.

#### Preparation

Read through the text, copying out four or five lines that are important to the content of the text.

#### Procedure

1 Dictate the lines you have chosen to the class in the order they appear in the text.
2 Ask the students to read the lines out loud. In a weaker class, you might wish to ask several students to read the same line. You can also write the lines on the board or ask a student to do this.
3 Ask the students to contemplate what the text will be about and accept any guesses. Students could attempt this in pairs first and only later make their contributions to the whole group.
4 Give each student a copy of the text (or give the page number if the text is in a book) and ask them to skim the text and find the dictated lines. They then underline these lines.

5 Ask individual students to read a line each and point out its position in the text. They should say, for example 'Number one is the third line from the bottom'.
6 Ask the students if they have changed their minds about the content of the text, and if so, what made them change their minds.
7 Begin the actual reading of the text. You might want to make this either silent reading or reading out loud, or perhaps a combination of the two.

**VARIATIONS**

i For capable and confident students you can dictate the lines in a scrambled order, then ask them to put them in what they perceive to be the correct order. If you have a very imaginative and proficient group, you can also ask them to compose a text of their own which includes these lines. Ask the students to read their newly-created texts out loud and discuss these briefly before they look at the 'real' text – the one you plan to read with them. Make sure that you praise their creativity. Student texts are sometimes more imaginative and interesting than those written by professionals!

ii For less capable students you can provide photocopies of the lines of text, rather than dictating them. You may also wish to underline these same lines in the complete text so that the students simply have to match the underlined lines with the ones you have given them on the handout. Very weak students can do the predicting activity in their native language.

iii You can also provide the lines in the native language, ask the students to translate them into English and then follow through with the predicting activity. This gets to be interesting when they start looking for the lines in the text, because their English versions will rarely be exactly the same as the versions in the original text.

# TREASURE HUNT

## 1.2

**MATERIALS**
One magazine or newspaper in the target language per student or per group

**LEVEL**
Elementary + (if there is a suitable student newspaper) or intermediate +

**SKILLS**
Skimming and scanning; Intra-group cooperation; Inter-group competition

**TIME**
15–25 minutes

**SUGGESTED TEXTS**
Daily newspaper or Student newspaper

*Treasure hunt* is an activity involving skimming and scanning which encourages both intra-group cooperation and inter-group competition. As groups work on their assigned tasks, some will quickly realise that they get better and faster results by assigning tasks to different individuals in the group. This is excellent cooperative group practice and should not be discouraged (See Step 5).

It is important that the students understand the concepts of skimming and scanning. Scanning means glancing through a text quickly in order to get the gist of the content. Skimming means glancing through the text quickly in order to find specific information. These techniques do not require in-depth reading, but are rather quick prereading exercises which help us to decide which parts of the text we will later choose to read with care.

## Preparation

1 Read through the entire newspaper looking for articles dealing with the same subject. Also look for interesting items found in headlines, under pictures, in first paragraphs or in easily-spotted texts. (You will need these for the bonus question). Make yourself a list of these, noting the headlines and page numbers.
2 Create a task sheet from the information you have gleaned, with about twelve items.
This is how it might look for a daily newspaper:

- Find two articles about economics. Give the headline and page number.
- Find three articles about education. Give the headline and page number.
- Find one article about fashion. Give the headline and page number.
- Where is the President of the United States this week?
- Who is the assistant editor of this paper?
- Why is the editor of the paper angry?
- Which book about animals is being reviewed?
- Who gave a large sum of money to the local hospital?
- Where was an election held?
- Where is there a demonstration?

In addition, prepare a few bonus questions on a separate list. You can use these for the groups that finish early.

## Procedure

1 Divide the class into groups of four or five. Allow them a few minutes to choose a name. You may, if you wish, give a category for these names, such as flowers, animals, sports teams, cities or rock groups. Set a time limit for this activity. Two minutes is usually sufficient.
2 Write the names of all the groups on the board. Comment on unusual or interesting names – praise creative effort!

3 Tell the class they will be practising skimming and scanning, reading techniques which both call for speed. Elicit or explain the meanings of the words *skim* and *scan*.

4 Appoint one student to be timekeeper, preferably someone who has a second hand on their watch and who needs a bit of extra attention.

5 Give out the newspapers or magazines and the task sheets. Tell the students that this is a contest between the groups. The group that finds the information on the task sheet first is the winner, but all other results will also be recorded.

Make sure that each group gets only one task sheet. This will encourage them to work together. If you give each individual a task sheet, they will be sitting in groups but working as individuals.

6 When the first group has finished, the timekeeper should note the time taken. You can hand them the extra bonus items that you prepared for this eventuality.

7 When all the groups have finished, ask them to report their results. This is the part that is fun and interesting because you are going to discover that the class has found different articles from you. Allow all the groups to contribute what they have found.

8 Let the class suggest which article looked particularly interesting and should be chosen for in-depth reading. Take a vote on the most popular article.

**VARIATION**

For less capable students you can use *Treasure hunt* as a prereading activity for a one-page text. The task sheet could include such items as:

Find all the words that start with 'F'.
Find three numbers on the page.
Find all the verbs in the past tense, etc.

## NEEDLE IN A HAYSTACK

**1.3**

**MATERIALS**
A task sheet for each group

**LEVEL**
Intermediate +

**SKILLS**
Skimming; Asking questions

**TIME**
15–20 minutes

**SUGGESTED TEXTS**
Long, fairly complex texts (magazines, newspapers or long articles)

*Needle in a haystack* is similar to Activity 1.2 *Treasure hunt*, but has additional components for more of a challenge. This is a good activity for bright students who enjoy outwitting a trick question on a test.

### Preparation

Look through the text for interesting details such as captions, key ideas in paragraphs, chapter headings, vital summaries, etc. Make a task sheet with five or six detailed questions. Here is how your task sheet might look:

1 Who takes responsibility on page 16?

2 What two place names are mentioned in Chapter 4?

3 Who is Harvey?

4 What is the last complete sentence in Chapter 18?

5 Where was this book published?

### Procedure

1 Ask the students to sit in groups of three. (See General techniques on page xiv for advice on grouping.) Give each group one task sheet and one copy of the text. (Having only one copy will encourage them to work together.)
2 Their job is to locate the answers to the questions on the task sheet as quickly as possible.
3 Remind them that the answers will be found more quickly if they work as a group.
4 As soon as one group has located the answers, declare the group 'tentative' winner. They will become the 'real' winner if all their answers are correct. Should they have made a mistake, the group which corrects them first and has all the answers becomes the winner.
5 If you want your group to move around, now is the time to ask them to sit with people they have not worked with previously. You could regroup by giving everyone a number, a letter, a colour or a fruit and asking them to sit with their own kind. If, on the other hand, you have a class that is working well, or one that needs quietening, ask them to remain in the same groups.
6 The task of each group is to make up three detailed questions on the text. The questions must be fairly similar to those you gave them on their task sheet, but they must, of course, not be the same as yours.

7 Stop the activity as soon as one group has finished.
8 Each group passes its questions to a neighbouring group which tries to answer them.
9 Bring the whole class together and ask each group to read out their own 'best' question and answer.
10 Tell the students that they will now start reading the text to see whether they had missed any interesting bits of information.

## 1.4 COMPARING QUOTATIONS

**MATERIALS**
A class set of texts

**LEVEL**
Higher intermediate +

**SKILLS**
Reading; Paraphrasing; Interpreting

**TIME**
15 minutes

**SUGGESTED TEXTS**
Essays or stories with a strong theme or message

All of us are occasionally inspired by the words of someone close or someone we admire. How many times have you caught yourself doing or not doing something because, 'Mother always used to say ...' A good friend of mine eases her worries by reminding herself, in the words of Franklin D Roosevelt, that 'There is nothing to fear but fear itself', and a young man I know bolsters his ambitions with Martin Luther King's 'I have a dream'.

This activity uses famous quotes as a route into a text.

### Preparation

Find three quotations suitable to the theme of the text or groups of texts to be studied.

For example, if you choose to read a passage on social responsibility with your class, you might use the following three quotations:

1 'Ask not what your country can do for you: ask what you can do for your country.' John F Kennedy
2 'No man is an Island entire of itself; every man is a piece of a continent, a part of the main.' John Donne
3 'The only thing necessary for the triumph of evil is for good men to do nothing.' Edmund Burke

### Procedure

1 Write the three quotations on the board and ask individual students to read them out loud. Each quotation should be read by more than one student.
2 Check that the students have understood the meaning of the quotations. Listen to any explanations offered, but do not add your own at this time.
3 Divide the class into small groups of four or five. In large classes where students sit in rows, pairs can turn to face other pairs in order to create foursomes.

   The task of these groups is to:

   i Choose one of the quotations on the board.

  **ii** Paraphrase it into simple English. For example, John Kennedy's quote could become 'Don't always wait for the government or some important people to fix whatever is wrong; think about how you and your friends could make things better.'

  **iii** Decide whether the quotation is relevant to their lives and their country today, and if so, give specific examples.

**4** When every group has finished, ask them to appoint a spokesperson who will report to the rest of the class. Note the most important or interesting conclusions on the board.

**5** Divide the class into two halves. If your class is small (fewer than twenty students) they can form two groups of ten each. If, on the other hand, you are working with a large class the activity can be done in pairs.

**6** Half of the class should decide what the three quotations have in common, while the other half decides how the quotations are different.

**7** Listen to their conclusions and try to deduce a common theme. Lead from this into the message of the passage you are about to read with bridge sentences, such as:

'We can see that all these quotations were about how and why we should care for other people. We are going to look at a passage which may tell us something similar. Let's see how it achieves this...'

(See General techniques on page xiv for ideas on using bridge sentences).

**NOTE**

It is a good idea to keep a list of interesting quotations. They come in handy as triggers for discussion and as prereading stimuli. There are many books of famous quotations on the market.

I have found, however, that my best gems in this department come from my own reading. I keep some index cards handy in the back of any book I am reading and when I come across something golden I copy it and later drop it in my teaching idea file under 'Q' for 'Quotations'. (See General techniques on page xiv for advice on keeping a file of ideas.)

## 1.5

**MATERIALS**
Bag or hat

**LEVEL**
Intermediate +

**SKILLS**
Vocabulary practice; Use of idioms

**TIME**
15–20 minutes

**SUGGESTED TEXTS**
Essays or articles with a strong thematic message

# FAKE QUOTATIONS

Not just the famous are quotable. All of us occasionally shine with words of wisdom. *Fake quotations* is an activity particularly suitable to creative classes. It allows the students to polish up their own verbal pearls and present them to the rest of the class. In this activity, students are asked to create their own quotations on a given theme – the same theme they will meet in the text. Students have come up with such gems as, 'Longing is better than fulfillment', 'Success saves struggle' and 'A frown might prevent a shout'.

## Procedure

1 Tell the students they will be reading a text that deals with a particular topic such as 'hard work', or 'loneliness', or 'friendship'. Ask them to create a 'quotation' (something someone famous might have said) about the subject. Their quotation should not be more than one or, at the most, two sentences long, and it *must* be connected to the given theme. Give them the ones quoted above as examples. They might work in pairs, or in groups of three, or individually, depending on the size and/or temperament of the group. Tell them that you are giving only three minutes for this activity, so that they are not to brood too long on the creation of their gems. They may make up one or several quotations.
2 Ask the students to write each homemade quotation on a single strip of paper. Collect these strips in a bag or hat.
3 Ask the students to sit in groups of four. Each group pulls four quotations from the hat.
4 Together with the class make a list on the board of ten well-known personalities.
5 In their small groups, the students choose one of the four quotations they have pulled out and attribute it to one of the famous personalities on the board. They should also decide when or why the personality made this statement.
6 Each group tells the rest of the class why they attributed the quotation to the person they chose. After each explanation, the real author may acknowledge authorship.
7 Use a bridge sentence such as: 'We have taken some time looking at the idea of ___________. Now we are going to read a text on this issue and see how it is dealt with there.'

## DEBATABLE QUOTATION

## 1.6

**MATERIALS**
A controversial quotation; paper clips

**LEVEL**
Intermediate +

**SKILLS**
Interpretation; Sustained speaking

**TIME**
15–20 minutes

**SUGGESTED TEXTS**
Stories, essays or poems on one theme

Controversy adds spice to a lesson. This activity leads into a text while keeping controversy pleasantly bubbling. The discussion does not become disjointed or rowdy because it has a focus.

### Preparation

Choose a somewhat controversial quotation which is tied to the text you are about to read.

### Procedure

1 Write the quotation on the board and underneath it write:

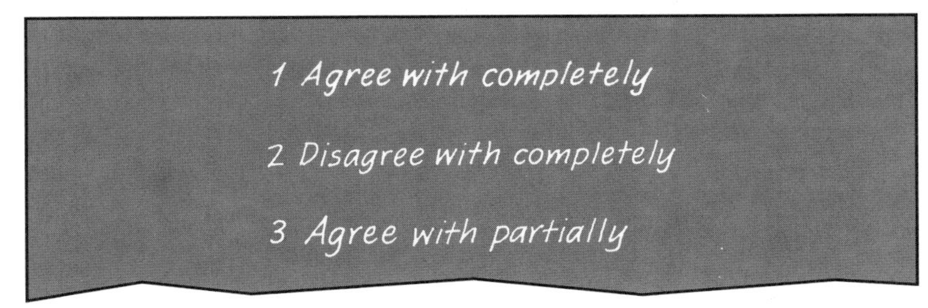


Fig. 1

2 Ask the students to write down whichever of these most closely expresses their own feelings.
3 Ask the students to tell each other, in pairs, which of the three they have chosen and why.
4 Bring the class together and ask, 'Has anyone heard anything particularly interesting from their partner while working in pairs?' Listen to and comment on the answers.
5 Ask the students to write 1, 2 or 3, depending on which statement they have chosen, on a piece of paper which they pin to themselves with a paper clip.
6 Tell the students to move about the room trying to find other people who have the same number. They then form groups of three and explain their choice to each other.
7 Ask the students to mingle again. This time their job is to find someone who has marked a different number. They try to convince each other of the rightness of their own position.
8 Invite three students, each representing a different point of view, to sit in front of the class. Their task is to present their views, panel-style, to the entire class. The class questions them about their views.
9 To approach the text, use a bridge sentence such as, 'We have heard many points of view about ______. We are now going to read a passage (article/story) which will agree with (disagree with/enlarge on) some of the things we have said.'

**NOTE**
In large, unruly classes Steps 5, 6 and 7 may be omitted.

**VARIATION**
If your text is difficult, take the debatable quotation from it. When the students reach this part in their actual reading, there will be a wonderful moment of recognition.

## 1.7 PLACING IT

**MATERIALS**
A class set of texts

**LEVEL**
Intermediate +

**SKILLS**
Dictation;
Skimming;
Comparing texts;
Predicting;
Sentence writing

**TIME**
10–15 minutes

**SUGGESTED TEXTS**
Narratives

The geographical setting of a passage often significantly influences the meaning of the text. In this activity students are asked to consider the importance of place. The activity involves guessing about where certain events might occur. The variety of guesses creates a lively interest in the lesson. Students have guessed that the passage below took place anywhere from Chicago to the surface of the moon and they have given good reasons for these different guesses too.

### Preparation

Choose a short passage from the text to be used as a class dictation. The passage must not mention the place where it is set.

### Procedure

1 Dictate a few lines from the text. These lines may contain any information except the place in which the passage is set. For example:

> And now the storm overtook him. He walked facing the cruel wind, straining his entire body to force it toward the earth, but the earth seemed eager to give him up. Pushing against the wind was like trying to struggle against stone walls closing in on him.

2 Ask students, in pairs or small groups, to decide where the passage is taking place and why the character is there. Tell them that they must give reasons for their guesses. For example, they might say, 'That could only happen in New York. The winds there are horrible!'
3 Elicit several suggestions from the groups.
4 Ask the students to add two more sentences to the passage and then read these out.
5 Tell them that you will read the text in which the passage appears. Give out the texts and ask them to skim it to locate the passage.

# OFF THE WALL

## 1.8

**MATERIALS**
Cards or slips of paper; Blu-tack or sellotape

**LEVEL**
Intermediate +

**SKILLS**
Asking questions; Dictation; Reading

**TIME**
10–15 minutes

**SUGGESTED TEXTS**
Any texts

This activity involves students milling about the room in pairs. I like using it when I feel that a class has grown tired of sitting down. It is especially useful in a two-hour block of lessons. If your class is a large, unruly one which must remain seated, you can simply supply the answers (Step 3) on a sheet of paper to each pair of students.

## Preparation

Take any short or medium length text and write about eight to twelve *Wh* questions about it. Write the answers to these questions on index cards or slips of paper. Stick these cards or slips of paper around the wall of your classroom before you start the activity. If you start the activity in the middle of a lesson, ask a student to stick up the cards while you are doing something else.

## Procedure

1 Dictate the questions to the class.
2 When the dictation is complete ask the students to walk around the room in pairs, trying to find at least five answers to the questions you have dictated. Set a time limit of about five to seven minutes for this stage. There will always be at least one pair which has all the answers by the time most of the pairs have only found five. It is useful to have a few extra cards to give these quick workers, or you can simply ask the students to take their seats as soon as the first pair has finished. Most of them will have five answers by then.
3 When the students have returned to their seats, elicit all the questions and answers.
4 Tell the students that the questions and answers relate to a passage they are about to read. Ask them if they have any more questions about this passage before they read it.
5 Listen to their questions and record some on the board. Ask the class to predict or imagine answers to these new questions.
6 Ask the class to predict the content of the article.
7 They read the text and check their predictions.

## 1.9

**MATERIALS**
Slips of paper; Blu-tack or sellotape

**LEVEL**
Elementary +

**SKILLS**
Reading; Predicting

**TIME**
5–15 minutes, depending on the size of the class

**SUGGESTED TEXTS**
Any text involving general knowledge or having in it some facts about which students have some previous knowledge

# WRITING ON THE WALL

This is a variation on the tried and tested 'true and false' technique which involves students in a milling phase. If you feel that your class is too large or undisciplined for such a walkabout, you could hand out a list of true/false statements instead.

## Preparation

Before the lesson construct a number of true or false statements relating to the text you are about to read. These questions should be the kind that will allow the students to guess at answers, but make sure that the answers are indeed provided by the text which they will read. Write these on cards or slips of paper.

If my text is based on diets and eating habits, the true and false statements might look like these:

- Food consciousness is going out of style
- Women are more concerned with slimness than men
- Anorexia is an eating disability disease
- Young children need a great deal of fat to be healthy

The number of statements should, ideally, be the same as the number of students in your class, but if you have a very large class, have at least one slip for each pair or trio.

## Procedure

1 Number the statements and stick them on the classroom wall.
2 Ask the students to walk around the room with a partner. Together they must read the statements and decide whether they are true or false. One of them should write down the number of each statement with a T or F next to it.
3 After they have read all the statements and marked them either T or F, each student (or in large classes, each pair) should take one of the sentences off the wall and return to their seat.
4 Ask the students to read their sentences out in order. Say, 'Who has number 1?' The student (or pair) who has taken down number 1 reads it and explains why it is marked true or false. Ask the class if they agree with their decision. This often brings about spirited discussion. Remember that the text has not yet been read and that they are guessing or using their general knowledge. Go through all the statements in this way.
5 Tell the students that they are about to read an article/story which might provide answers to some of the questions brought up in the discussion.

ACKNOWLEDGEMENT
*Off the wall* and *Writing on the wall* are variations of an activity I learned in a workshop given by Kevin Keating of the Center of English as a Second Language at the University of Arizona, Tucson, Arizona.

## CLOSE THE GAP

## 1.10

**MATERIALS**
Sheets of paper

**LEVEL**
Intermediate +

**SKILLS**
Predicting; Making outlines; Asking questions

**TIME**
10–15 minutes

**SUGGESTED TEXTS**
Short fiction

There seems to be a human tendency to want to fill spaces and close gaps. You have probably experienced this yourself when filling out a form. Even when we tell ourselves that we want to read through the whole form before marking any of the blanks, we find ourselves almost irresistibly filling the spaces. *Close the gap*, a prereading guessing technique, exploits this tendency.

### Preparation

Before the lesson, write the first sentence of the story you are going to read at the top of a sheet of paper and the last sentence of the story at the bottom of the same sheet. Photocopy one sheet for each small group of students.

### Procedure

1 Divide the class into small groups and give each group the sheet you have prepared. Make sure that, in addition to the paper which you have given them, each group also has extra paper to write on.
2 Tell the students that what they see on the sheet are the first and last sentences of the story they are about to read. Their task is to fill the blank in the middle.
3 Ask each group to appoint a secretary. Explain that filling in the blank will involve three stages:
   i First, the group brainstorm for ideas while the secretary writes them down.
   ii Next, they organise the ideas and make an outline of the summary that has resulted.
   iii Finally, the group writes a summary of the story they have predicted.
4 Walk around helping them through the various stages.
5 Ask each group to read their summary out loud. Praise creative efforts. At the end of each reading, encourage listening students to ask questions about this version of the story.

# CHAPTER 2

# *Perceive and ponder*

## *Using visuals and visualisations*

A picture, we are told, is worth a thousand words. But we have also heard of the power of the word. This chapter attempts to combine the verbal with the visual.

**2.1**

**MATERIALS**
Large sheets of newsprint paper; felt pens or crayons

**LEVEL**
Intermediate +

**SKILLS**
Describing; Predicting

**TIME**
10–15 minutes

**SUGGESTED TEXTS**
Short stories or essays

## THE MENTAL VIDEO

This is an excellent activity for imaginative classes and teachers. Particularly suitable for fiction texts, it insists that students create their own mental picture of an object prior to encountering it in the textual setting.

### Preparation

Choose a story or essay in which an object plays a significant part and appears quite early in the text. This can be any object – a house, a park bench, a hat, a book – anything, provided it is of significance in the text.

### Procedure

1 Ask the students to close their eyes and visualise the object you have decided on. Ask them to imagine its size, its colour, the materials it is made of, how it is displayed and how it is used. If this is relevant to your object, ask them to imagine its price and location. If any sound is associated with the object, ask students if they can hear it. Before you proceed ask, 'Do you see your ______ very clearly? Nod your heads if you do, please.'
2 Ask the students to imagine a person approaching this object and using it in some way.
3 In pairs, the students tell each other about this scene on their mental video.
4 Let the whole class listen to a few descriptions reported by partners who heard them. Ask, 'Did anyone hear a particularly interesting description? Susan, could you tell us about David's ______?'
5 Elicit general qualities of such objects and make a list on the board. For example, if you are talking about hats, ask what their function is, how you use them, what they are made of, etc.

6 At this point, you can do either of the following.
  i Ask the students to skim the text silently until they locate the object in the text. Compare the account in the text with the students' image. These comparisons can be made first in groups and later reported to the whole class.
  ii Tell the students that the text they are about to read features such an object. Ask them to predict what the text might be about.
7 In groups, the students make a poster featuring either the object that appears in the text or the object as they imagined it.
8 Once completed, display the posters on the classroom walls.

**NOTE**
I did this exercise using a story by Flannery O'Connor called, 'Everything That Rises Must Converge'. In this story a hideous hat serves as a focus for symbolic meaning.

I asked students to visualise a hat and got everything from cowboy hats to turbans, with extremely fanciful constructions in between. When I asked them to think about what their visualised hats were made of, I got feathers, veils, felt, straw, velvet, beads, brim etc. Students can give these details in their native language if you or other students are able, at some stage, to offer reliable translations.

In the story, the hat is green and purple and looks like a cushion with its stuffing out. The posters later made of this object (Step 7) were exceedingly colourful and we displayed them on the classroom walls.

## GATES

**2.2**

**MATERIALS**
None

**LEVEL**
Intermediate +

**SKILLS**
Predicting; Describing

**TIME**
10–15 minutes

**SUGGESTED TEXTS**
Stories, essays or articles

A gate is always a good object for visualisation. I ask my students to see the size, colour and design of the gate. What materials is it made of? How does one close or open it? I ask them to imagine themselves walking through this gate. Then I ask them to describe who or what is on the other side. I tell them that any new text is the opening of a gate. I give them a few hints about what will be behind this particular gate we are about to open and ask them to predict what they will find, before we start reading.

### Procedure

1 Ask the students to close their eyes and imagine a gate. Ask them to consider the size of the gate, its colour, and what it is made of. Give them time to form the visualisation. Ask: 'Do you see your gate clearly?' They should answer by nodding but keep their eyes closed.
2 Ask them to continue the visualisation by seeing themselves opening the gate and walking through to the other side. Ask, 'What is there to see on the other side?' Give them time to picture this.

3 Ask them to share their mental pictures of the gate and what was beyond it in pairs.
4 Give them a few details from the text you are about to read. These need not be central details, but they must be interesting enough to facilitate guessing. For example, 'We are going to read about crocodiles from the point of view of a scientist. What do you think the scientist might wish to tell us about them?'
5 In pairs, the students brainstorm the possible development of the text.
6 In plenary, ask them to report their guesses, and invite questions.

## 2.3 I'M IN THE PICTURE

**MATERIALS**
Pictures of scenery without people such as postcards, or pictures from travel magazines. At least one picture per student

**LEVEL**
Intermediate +

**SKILLS**
Speaking; Listening; Describing

**TIME**
15–20 minutes

**SUGGESTED TEXTS**
Narratives in which setting or scene are crucial and perhaps described in detail

In this activity, students imagine they enter a picture. They then share what they experience there.

### Preparation

Find suitable pictures and bring them to class.

### Procedure

1 Spread out the pictures where they can be seen by the whole class. This can be done on your desk in a small class or on the central floor space in an average size class. In very large classes, I have asked students to sit in groups of four (pair facing pair) and given each foursome six pictures.
2 Ask the students to choose, with their eyes only, the picture in which they would like to be a visitor.
3 Ask the students to actually pick up their chosen picture, but if someone else has made the same choice, they are to graciously withdraw and make another choice. Tell them this is an exercise in compromise.
4 Students now form groups of three. In these groups each student shows their picture to an audience of two and explains why they chose that particular picture. It is the task of the two listeners to respond by saying something positive to the speaker either about the picture or about the remarks the speaker has made. The comments must be specific and positive. For example, a student might say: 'I really didn't like the picture you chose when I first saw it, but now that you have explained how it reminds you of your wonderful trip to Switzerland, I am beginning to like it too.'

5 With the whole class, discuss why we like to visit certain places. Tell them that in the text they are about to read a certain place (or places) is described. Give them a few details of this place and ask the students to predict more of the content of the text.

**NOTE**
I have found this activity fosters a happier class climate. By asking students to validate or support each other's choices, you encourage them to compliment each other in a way so often needed but so seldom found in a school setting.

ACKNOWLEDGEMENT
This exercise is an adaptation of one I learned from Dr Ora Zohar of the Teaching Improvement Center at the Hebrew University, Jerusalem, Israel.

# FACES

## 2.4

**MATERIALS**
Pictures of faces

**LEVEL**
Intermediate +

**SKILLS**
Describing; Story-telling; Asking questions; Writing

**TIME**
15 minutes

**SUGGESTED TEXTS**
Any text in which people feature prominently

How do we form impressions of people? Are our first impressions usually right or wrong? What is it about the way someone looks which attracts or repels us? These questions are considered as we approach a text by looking at some faces. I have used this activity as an introduction to 'Richard Corey', a poem by Edwin Arlington Robinson. The poem describes a much admired, highly respected, good looking, well educated and rich denizen of a small town. The inhabitants of the town, who are enormously jealous of Richard Corey, never get over the shock they receive when the much envied Corey, one quiet summer's night, commits suicide. Our impressions of people are indeed often wrong.

## Preparation

Bring lots of pictures of faces to the lesson. The greater the number and variety of faces the better, but there must be at least one face for each student.

## Procedure

1 Spread out the pictures where they can be seen by the whole class. This can be done on your desk in a small class or on the central floor space in an average size class. In very large classes, I have asked students to sit in groups of four (pair facing pair) and given each foursome six pictures.

2 Ask students to choose, with their eyes only, the face which they find most appealing. Sometimes I ask classes to choose the face which they feel they could befriend.
3 After a wait of five seconds or so ask students to pick up their chosen picture.
4 Allow everyone to study the face they have chosen for a few seconds. Then ask them to make certain decisions about this person and to write down their conclusions. They give the person they have chosen a name, an age and an occupation. They also imagine an important event that has occurred recently in the life of this person.
5 In groups of three, students now introduce their people to each other. They might say, for example: 'I want you to meet Andrea Lewis. She is thirty-two years old and works as a secretary. Recently she has met the man she wants to marry and now her only problem is that she must convince him that she is indeed the woman he has been waiting for.' The other two students ask the speaker questions to discover more about the person. Each student finds out all they can about their partners' people.
6 Bring the whole group together and discuss their reasons for choosing a particular face. Ask, 'Why are we attracted to certain people?' Elicit several answers.
7 Tell them that they are about to read a text in which people are important. Give a few details and ask the class to guess what kind of people they will meet in the text.

ACKNOWLEDGEMENT
This exercise is a variation of a technique I first learned from Dr Ora Zohar of the Teaching Improvement Center at the Hebrew University, Jerusalem, Israel.

## NATURE WALK

## 2.5

**MATERIALS**
A recording of soothing background music is helpful but not essential

**LEVEL**
Intermediate +

**SKILLS**
Listening

**TIME**
5–10 minutes

**SUGGESTED TEXTS**
Texts on any aspect of nature, ecology or nature preservation

*Nature walk* is a visualisation which provides an extremely relaxing entry into a text. I have found this activity particularly useful at the end of a difficult day or after my students have experienced a taxing physical education lesson. Adolescent learners love to let their imaginations go and play games. But they are at an age where admitting as much is anathema. This is why any game-like activity must always be introduced as an important and serious matter so, when starting this activity, I tell my classes that it is a technique derived from Suggestopedia (which indeed it is). I tell them that learning languages through Suggestopedia has been very effective and that it requires a state of relaxation which we will practise in the activity.

### Preparation

Practise telling the stories below in a soothing voice. It is better to tell them than to read them, so learn them well.

### Procedure

1 As soon as your students have entered the classroom, tell them that you know they are tired, so you want them to sit down and relax. Ask them to close their eyes and listen to the music. If you have no music, ask them to listen to a peaceful, dark silence. Interestingly, I have discovered that the activity works best if I also close my eyes. That way, if anyone sneaks a look around, they will see that I, too, am involved and that I am not watching everyone.
2 In a soft voice begin the nature walk. Here are two possible texts to read to the class:

A walk on the beach

It is late afternoon on the long, low sandy beach, but it is still very warm. As you walk barefoot on the sand, you can feel the pleasant warmth of the sun caressing your shoulders. The sand feels soft and warm as it gives way beneath your feet. In the distance seagulls are calling to each other. There is a soft splash of the waves gently breaking against the shore. You lie down in the sand, feeling the softness of the sand as it gently receives the contours of your body. You stretch in the sand and feel the sun enveloping you in lukewarm comfort. Slowly you get up and move towards the water. The water bubbles up around your feet. You feel good and at peace with the universe. Open your eyes slowly and gently. You feel relaxed and refreshed and ready to tackle a challenging task of reading a new article in English.

A walk in the woods

It is an early morning in the spring. You are walking in a green leafy forest on a well-trodden path. Rays of sun filter through the lacy leafwork above you. You walk quietly, well aware of the birdsong all about you. The path below your feet grows mossy and soon you are walking on a soft carpet of moss. Somewhere nearby a brook gurgles. Suddenly the leafy greenness of the woods opens up into a sunny meadow. It is a green field dotted with blue and yellow flowers, butterflies hover over it and at the edge of the meadow you see the soft form of a young deer. You stand very still so as not to disturb the animal, but this stillness is not difficult for you. It is a relaxed stillness and you feel part of everything around you. You are rested and relaxed. It is time to return to the class where you will feel refreshed and ready to cope with an interesting new text in English.

3 When you see that everyone is alert, start reading the text. Don't worry, no one will fall asleep on you!

**NOTE**
See page 117 for further reading on Suggestopedia.

## 2.6

**MATERIALS**
A number of 'shop window lists' to be put up on the walls of your classroom; Blu-tack or sellotape; paper clips or pins

**LEVEL**
Intermediate +

**SKILLS**
Reading; Fluency practice; Discussion

**TIME**
10–15 minutes

**SUGGESTED TEXTS**
Any essay or article which presents a clear point of view on a subject

## THE SHOP WINDOW LIST

I like this activity because it appears to have a very structured framework, yet it offers endless possibilities for compromise and adjustment.

### Preparation

Make a list with ten clear statements of opinion related to the subject which your reading text deals with. These statements may agree or disagree with the point of view of the writer, but they should express some point of view. If your text deals with travel, your list might look as follows:

1. Travel broadens one's outlook on life.
2. Travel is tiring.
3. One should never travel to foreign countries until one has seen one's own country.
4. Most people enjoy travel.
5. Although most people don't admit it, they really don't enjoy travel.
6. Travel is terribly expensive.
7. Never travel alone!
8. Travel is dangerous.
9. You always meet interesting people when you travel.
10. Never travel with small children.

Stick several such lists on the walls of your classroom before the beginning of the lesson.

## Procedure

1 Tell the students that all the lists stuck on the walls are identical. The lists are shop windows from which they must choose displayed items. Give out one paper clip or pin to each student. Keep extra paper clips or pins in a handy box. Some students invariably lose theirs. Ask everyone to get up and look over any one of the lists. They should take paper and pen with them. Their job is to find three statements with which they agree. Tell them that if a statement comes very close to something they agree or disagree with they may make a small change in it just to clarify a point of view. This adds flexibility and interest as students will usually remove the 'never' and the 'always'.

2 Once they have found their three statements, ask them to write the numbers of the statements on a piece of paper and pin this piece of paper to their clothing. A student might, for example, walk about marked '6, 2, 8'.

3 Their task now is to move around the room looking for other students who have written at least two of the same numbers. They tell each other why they agree with these statements, and whether they have changed anything and why.

4 When they have done this, ask the students to find someone who has not written any of their numbers. Once they have found such a person, they must convince them of the 'rightness' of at least one of their own statements and in turn listen to the point of view of the other person. The mingling here is lively and interesting because students must often return to check the lists. Since they are wandering around with just numbers, not statements, they will have forgotten the statements and will have to double-check, often changing their minds as they do so.

5 Tell the students that they will now read a text which relates to the subject they have been discussing.

### VARIATION

This activity works best when you want your students to move around. If you have a difficult class that needs to be kept seated, simply give each individual a list rather than sticking them up around the classroom, and allow your students to hold their discussions in pairs.

## 2.7 THE SURREALISTIC PAINTING

**MATERIALS**
An interesting picture that can be connected to your text

**LEVEL**
Intermediate +

**SKILLS**
Predicting; Asking questions; Making notes

**TIME**
10–15 minutes

**SUGGESTED TEXTS**
Any text which deals with existentialist dilemmas, memories, the unreal, flashbacks, etc.

In the surrealist world nothing is taken for granted. Reality and fantasy intermingle. Dreams are forever interrupting life. I have found that surrealistic pictures, particularly those of René Magritte, stimulate the imagination and serve well as affective introductions to both fiction and non-fiction texts. You can make the connection between text and picture very free and loose in the same way that surrealistic paintings work.

For example, I have used Magritte's 'La Reproduction Interdite' (the famous painting of a correct young man with his back turned to us looking into the mirror in which we see, amazingly, the reflection of his back rather than his front) as an introduction to James Joyce's 'Eveline' (about a person who never knows her own worth and therefore does not see her own face). I have also used this painting to introduce a non-fiction passage on learning to drive since driving is for many teenagers a symbol of growing up – finding their identity (their face) in the world.

### Preparation

Bring to the lesson an interesting picture that is large enough for the whole class to see.

### Procedure

1. Show the picture to the class. If the picture is not large enough to be seen from the back of the room, walk around with it, making sure everyone has had a good look.
2. Put the picture away and ask students to write down anything they remember having seen in it.
3. Ask them to share what they have seen in pairs.
4. Ask one pair to report what they have seen. Ask the rest of the class to add items omitted by this pair.
5. Show the picture again.
6. Put the picture away and ask the class to report any details they missed the first time.
7. Show the picture again and ask, 'What questions can we ask ourselves about this picture?'
8. Allow the students a couple of minutes to write down questions. Continue displaying the picture.
9. Ask everyone to read out their questions.
10. Tell them that you will now read a text that made you think of this picture. Ask them to imagine their own pictures as they read the text.
11. After the text has been read through, ask the students, in pairs, to brainstorm connections between the text and the picture.

# MAKING CONNECTIONS

This is a competitive, brainstorming activity that can be fun provided the pace and timing is right. Everything must be done at a rather brisk pace or the whole thing drags. The greater the variety of pictures you use, the more interesting this activity becomes.

## Preparation

Bring a variety of pictures to the lesson. There should be at least one for each group and a few extras.

## Procedure

1 Divide your class into small groups of five or six. Allow each group to give itself a name or number the groups yourself.
2 Give each group a picture.
3 Tell them that they are going to read a passage on a topic which you will name later and that their task will be to try, as quickly as possible, to make as many connections as they can between the topic and the picture.
4 Demonstrate what you mean by holding up a picture, naming a topic and giving several connections. You could, for example hold up a picture of a house and say, 'My topic is Africa. Let's see how can I connect Africa with this house. Well, I can think of housing in Africa, homelessness in Africa, change of architectural styles in Africa, the family structure in Africa, use of wood in Africa, etc...' Tell them that their connections can be as far-fetched as they wish, but that each connection must be explained somehow. The group that has the most connections will win.
5 Ask each group to appoint a secretary who will make notes of the connections.
6 Tell the students they have four minutes from the time you give the topic. Appoint a timekeeper to call 'time-up' after the four minutes.
7 Ask the class if they are ready.
8 Announce the topic and write it on the board.
9 If after about thirty seconds, you see a group which seems hopelessly stuck, quickly give them another picture and signal them to go on.
10 After the timekeeper has stopped the class, elicit all the connections. Make sure that each group holds up their picture while giving the connections. The class may challenge any connection which seems weak to them and it is up to the group to justify and explain their connection. If they are unable to do this, the connection doesn't count. The group with most unchallenged connections wins.
11 Students begin reading the text. Ask them to find any information linking up with their earlier discussion.

## 2.8

**MATERIALS**
Interesting pictures

**LEVEL**
Intermediate +

**SKILLS**
Fluency practice; Predicting; Making notes

**TIME**
15–20 minutes

**SUGGESTED TEXTS**
Any fiction or non-fiction text

## 2.9

**MATERIALS**
None

**LEVEL**
Intermediate +

**SKILLS**
Explaining; Fluency practice

**TIME**
10–15 minutes

**SUGGESTED TEXTS**
Any fiction text with clear examples of symbolic meaning

# PICTURE A SYMBOL

Symbols evoke powerful images which stir our emotions and move us to action. I have found that this introductory activity using symbols works well in thoughtful classes which have had some time to warm up together.

You may wish to discuss the use of literary symbols with your class. (Symbol: an object, picture or word which stands for something else besides its everyday meaning.) Symbols add depth and meaning to a text and are always firmly rooted in reality. For example, in the story 'The Blind Man' by D H Lawrence, a storm rages. The storm fits very naturally into the English setting of the story, but it is also a symbol of the inner turmoil in the lives of the three characters. Or, in the well-known story of *Cinderella*, the prince insists on marrying the girl whose tiny foot will fit perfectly into the little glass slipper left at the palace. This fits very well into the plot of the story but, on a symbolic level, the story tells us about the position of women in society. Small feet stand for a small helpless person who will have to be aided as she walks through life. It is perhaps worthwhile to point out that symbols may mean different things to different readers.

## Procedure

1 Write the word *symbol* on the board and ask the class if they know what the word means.
2 Elicit from the class some common symbols and their meanings. For example: a flag stands for country; money represents wealth; a wedding ring represents marriage; a dove represents peace, etc.
3 Ask each student to draw something which has symbolic meaning to them or that has been used symbolically in life, in history, in movies, on television or in books. Their drawings can be very simple. Demonstrate on the board. For example, draw a circle and explain that to you the circular shape stands for a pie which symbolises your mother's excellent cooking and makes you homesick.
4 Encourage students to show and discuss their symbols in small groups.
5 Tell them that they are going to read a story in which symbols are used and ask them to look for these as they proceed with their reading.

# PICTURE A PROCESS

2.10

**MATERIALS**
Cartoons from a newspaper

**LEVEL**
Intermediate +

**SKILLS**
Explaining; Asking questions

**TIME**
10–15 minutes

**SUGGESTED TEXTS**
Any text that describes a process

Recent books on teaching writing to speakers of other languages often include sections or articles about how one thing gradually, through a certain process, changes into something else. Cartoon drawings which move from square to square are natural visualisations of such a process.

## Preparation

Cut out some cartoons from a local newspaper. These could well be in the students native language.

## Procedure

1 Put the word 'process' on the board and ask if anyone knows what it means. Listen to explanations. (Process: a cumulative activity in which one action prepares for and leads up to the next with the result as a final product.)
2 Ask the students to think of some processes in their own lives. They may suggest such processes as getting ready for school in the morning, doing homework, baking a cake, etc.
3 Ask students to draw a cartoon of this process in four to six squares. The characters may speak through speech bubbles. The drawings can be done individually or in pairs. Display some of the cartoons you have brought and leave them out so that students may refer to them as they do their own drawing. Tell them that they only have five minutes for this task.
4 After five minutes, ask the students to explain their cartoons to each other in small groups.
5 Ask each group to choose its best cartoon to explain to the entire class. The class may ask questions of the artist after each explanation.
6 Tell them that they will read an article that deals with a process.

**NOTE**
I first started using this activity when I had a student who was excellent at drawing stick figures. He taught us all how to draw stick figures well. Once we had learned this skill, it was great fun to draw all kinds of cartoons. You might have such an artist in your class too. Why not ask?

## CHAPTER 3

# *See, select and suggest*

## *Utilising common objects*

Why is it so difficult for use to throw things away? Could it be that, once lived with, an object takes on aspects of ourselves and thus in disposing of it, we toss a bit of ourselves away? This chapter suggests how to exploit this magical relationship between people and things.

**3.1**

**MATERIALS**
Any object

**LEVEL**
Elementary +

**SKILLS**
Asking questions; Predicting

**TIME**
10–15 minutes

**SUGGESTED TEXTS**
Literary texts, either poetry or prose

### THE SURPRISE PACKAGE

This is an activity which takes advantage of the fact that the average classroom is a sterile setting in which chalk, board and textbooks rule. In such a setting, even a teapot, if handled correctly, becomes something unusually cosy – or even exotic. The activity invariably works well with both younger students and adult learners, but is not effective with teenagers unless the teacher has established a climate of 'playful' learning.

#### Preparation

Find an object which you can in some way connect to your text. It need not be an object that actually appears in the text. It simply has to be something that you can link to your text somehow, be it ever so impressionistically.
For example:

- A teapot for a text on how tea is grown.
- A wooden horse for a passage on home industries.
- An interesting bottle for a text on magic (genii from bottles).
- An ashtray for a passage about someone who gives up smoking, etc.

Wrap your object in several layers of newspaper.

#### Procedure

1 Bring the wrapped object to the lesson and tell your students that a stranger has left this package in your place in the staffroom. You are a bit afraid to unwrap it. What could it possibly be? Invite guesses.
2 Take off a few layers of paper and invite more guesses. Ask, 'Should I continue? Could someone be playing a trick on me?'
3 Reveal the object and express surprise. Invite the class to ask questions about or speculate on the object.

4 Link the object to the text through a bridge sentence or bridging questions. For example, suppose that the text you are about to teach is the fairy tale, *Cinderella*, and that your students have not read it before. The object you chose for your pretext activity is an old plimsoll or gym shoe. You have gone through the process of unwrapping and the plimsoll is theatrically revealed. There is some laughter. You might say:
'A plimsoll! What do you know! Who could have possibly left that? (looking plimsoll over carefully) Let's see, what is this shoe made of? (material, cloth, rubber, canvas) What do we use this kind of shoe for? (running, exercising, etc.) What are shoes usually made of? (leather) Now, we are going to read a story in which a shoe plays a very important role. It's a special shoe and it's made of glass. Could someone ask me a question about that shoe – a question that might help us to decide what the story we are going to read will be about?'
The students might ask, 'Whose shoe is it?' 'Why is it important in the story?', etc.

5 Answer the questions briefly, leaving room for mystery, and then ask the students to predict the plot of the story.

**VARIATION**

If you can't find an object that relates to your text, bring any object and ask your pupils to create the connection, you'll be amazed what can happen! For example:

| | |
|---|---|
| Teacher | Here is an old watch. We are going to read a passage about crocodiles. What possible connection can there be between a watch and crocodiles? |
| Student 1 | Watchbands are made from crocodile skin. |
| Student 2 | In a short time there won't be any crocodiles left in the world. |
| Student 3 | The crocodile is slow just like an old watch. |
| Student 4 | This watch was eaten by a crocodile and found in his stomach. The crocodile must have bitten off the whole hand! |
| Teacher | Those are all interesting suggestions. What else do you know about crocodiles? (Allows time for answers) Let's see what the text says. |

## 3.2

## MAKING CHOICES

**MATERIALS**
A bag full of small objects found around the average household, such as clothes pegs, small bottles, matches, decorative objects, bars of soap, a small torch, a medicine bottle, a plaster, a teaspoon, etc.

**LEVEL**
Elementary +

**SKILLS**
Fluency practice; Translation; Predicting

**TIME**
10–15 minutes

**SUGGESTED TEXTS**
Any text

*Making choices* is basically a brainstorming activity using objects as its trigger. I have found that it works best with younger learners or adult learners. With teenagers, I explain that this technique has been used to expand the imagination of workers in American industry. Indeed, I first learned about a variation of the technique from an article on business training in an American national magazine. All this seems to infuse the activity with enough seriousness to permit the teenage students to play.

### Preparation

Locate enough small objects for every student to have one each, put them in an opaque bag and bring it to the lesson.

### Procedure

1 Walk around the class with your bag and ask students to reach in, without looking and pull out any object their hand falls on. Some like to feel around in the bag before deciding. This adds some fun, so do allow for it.
2 Ask the students to sit in groups of three. (In large unruly classes where you don't want any moving about, put them in pairs.) Their task is to choose one of the three (or two) objects to become the group's or pair's special object. Tell them that this must be done quickly and do not allow more than one minute for it.
3 Ask each group or pair to explain to the whole class why they chose one object over another. In elementary classes permit the use of the native language and then ask the help of the rest of the class to translate what they have said into the target language.
4 Ask the students to brainstorm for any topics that might be associated with the particular object they are holding. For example, a teaspoon might be associated with sugar, tea, feeding babies, the metal industry, table manners, diets, cooking, etc.
5 Ask each group to read their list out to the class. Before they read it out, they should hold up the object they have chosen. In elementary classes I again allow the use of the native language and then try to elicit translations to the target language from more knowledgeable students. In very large classes I do not listen to each group or pair, but, instead, ask them to form groups of six and report to each other. Later each group tells the whole class the list which they chose as the most interesting.
6 Tell your students that you are about to read an article about a particular topic. Ask them to make a connection between that topic and any of the objects that have been displayed.

ACKNOWLEDGEMENT
This technique is a variation of one I learned from Dr Ora Zohar of the Teaching Improvement Center at the Hebrew University, Jerusalem, Israel.

## MEANINGFUL OBJECT

## 3.3

**MATERIALS**
None

**LEVEL**
Intermediate +

**SKILLS**
Fluency practice; Predicting

**TIME**
10–15 minutes

**SUGGESTED TEXTS**
Fiction or non-fiction text in which an object features prominently

This is an introspective activity which allows students to get to know each other better. It works best when the text features a significant object. I used this activity to introduce a section of 'Eveline' by James Joyce. It was the part of the story in which Eveline dusted three objects. She had dusted these objects for as long as she could remember and had always wondered where the dust came from. The objects were a picture of an absent priest, a print of a self-sacrificing saint and a broken harmonium. All symbolise problems in Eveline's life.

### Procedure

1 Ask the students to remember an object that has been meaningful to them. Perhaps it was a present they once got, perhaps it was a special purchase or maybe something they decided to give away. I show them my wedding ring and tell them how meaningful this ring, that I have worn for thirty-two years, is to me. I give them several seconds to consider and ask them to nod once they have thought of such an object.
2 In pairs or groups of three, the students describe their objects to each other and explain why these objects are or were meaningful to them.
3 Tell them that they are about to read a text which also features a meaningful object. Tell them what the object is.
4 In groups of three, students brainstorm for all the possible ways in which the object might figure in the text.
5 Elicit all the possibilities and begin reading the text. If the object appears early in the text, you can ask students to read silently until they encounter it and then read the paragraph it appears in out loud.

## 3.4

**MATERIALS**
A large plate or tray on which are displayed around 15 disparate small objects

**LEVEL**
Intermediate +

**SKILLS**
Speaking;
Predicting

**TIME**
10–15 minutes

**SUGGESTED TEXTS**
Any fiction or non-fiction text

# KIM'S GAME

This memory testing activity was originally based on a game described in *Kim* by Rudyard Kipling. I have found the activity suitable for those students who enjoy remembering detail as well as for the imaginative ones who like inventing stories. I also like the activity because it moves smoothly from individual work to pairwork to groupwork.

## Preparation

Find about fifteen disparate small objects such as, buttons, paper clips, matches, plasters, a small light bulb, a spool of thread, a box of matches, a pencil, etc. Bring them to class together with a plate on which they can be displayed and a napkin or cloth with which they can be covered.

## Procedure

1 Display the objects on the plate. Walk around the class with the plate and make sure that everyone has had a good look at them. Students may ask to look at the plate as many times as they wish but they may not write anything down.
2 Cover the plate.
3 Ask the students to write down, from memory, as many objects as possible from the plate. This is to be done individually. Keep a bilingual dictionary handy so that students can look up words they don't recall in the target language.
4 Uncover the plate and allow the students another look.
5 The students try to extend their list, but this time they do it in pairs and their responses must be more specific. They must state the colour and size of the objects. For example, a *small* spool of *green* thread, *three large brown* buttons, etc.
6 Allow the students to check the plate again. This time elicit forgotton objects from the whole class. Write these on the board.
7 Ask the students to sit in small groups, and write the first sentence of a story which includes at least one of the listed objects.
8 In plenary, ask a representative from each group to read the group's sentence to the rest of the class.
9 Tell them that they are going to read a text about ______. Ask them to write a second sentence in their story which includes the topic mentioned. When everyone has finished, ask each group to read their two sentences out loud.

# BOTH WAYS

## 3.5

**MATERIALS**
6–8 objects that can be clearly displayed in front of a class

**LEVEL**
Intermediate +

**SKILLS**
Speaking; Listening

**TIME**
10–15 minutes

**SUGGESTED TEXTS**
Any text dealing with a controversial issue

This activity works beautifully as a prereading exercise to a controversial reading passage. Instead of allowing students to become heated with the clear vision of their own point of view and then, as often happens in the case of teenager learners, grow rowdy and unpleasant, the activity helps to channel students' thinking into the observation of an issue from several angles.

## Preparation

Find six to eight objects that can be displayed in front of the class. These can be any objects. I have used a teddy bear, a wooden turtle, an old alarm clock, a sewing kit, a kettle, an old typewriter, an egg-slicer. Anything will do. You'll just have to try it to believe me!

## Procedure

1 Arrange the objects in a place where they can easily be seen by the whole class.
2 Ask each student to choose one object and make a list of either all its positive or all its negative attributes. Demonstrate first with an example of your own. (See Note below.)
3 In pairs, the students tell each other about their object and its attributes. Make them study their own list before they talk with a partner. Once they start, they should talk and not read from their list.
4 After both students have talked about their list and listened to their partner's list, they must provide the opposite opinion to everything their partner said. For example, if Student A has talked about how marvellous a teddy bear is, Student B should talk about what a useless toy it is, etc. Should both of them have chosen the same object and both spoken in its favour, they must together make out the opposition argument.
5 Tell the class that any issue can be seen from several points of view and that you are about to read an article which presents a certain point of view which they may agree or disagree with. Ask them to keep the opposition arguments in mind as they read the article.

### NOTE

I used this technique as a prereading exercise for a passage dealing with the controversial issue of population control. My object was a tomato. I happened to have brought one for my lunch that day. Holding up the tomato in front of my class, I began to sing its praises.

'The tomato is a magnificent vegetable,' I said. 'Look how beautiful, red and glossy it is! It is full of vitamin C. It has hardly any calories. It is juicy and a joy to bite into. When combined with other foods it helps to bring out their flavour. No wonder it has been called a "love apple". Oh, you wonderful tomato!'

Turning the tomato around and looking at it carefully, I changed my expression to one of total disgust.

'The tomato is a dreadful vegetable,' I said. 'No matter how carefully I wrap it, it always get squashed in my bag and makes the rest of my lunch into a mess. Of course, I would never eat it, except that my doctor forces me to do so. The stupid thing has no taste at all. When you bite into it you dribble all over your chin and your clothes. Of course, it provides no real nourishment whatsoever. The thing has hardly any calories. If you slice it up in a sandwich, it makes the bread soggy. Whoever invented tomatoes?'

## 3.6 HOW MUCH?

**MATERIALS**
None

**LEVEL**
Intermediate +

**SKILLS**
Speaking; Listening; Using the third conditional; Predicting

**TIME**
10–15 minutes

**SUGGESTED TEXTS**
Any dealing with money or financial issues

This is a useful prereading activity for any fiction or non-fiction reading selection which deals with financial problems, budgeting or money. I used it to get my students to predict the contents of a story by Dorothy Parker called 'The Standard of Living'. In it two office girls play a game in which they pretend to be heiresses to a fortune.

### Procedure

1. Ask the students, in pairs, to make a list of ten expensive objects, such as diamonds, mansions, yachts, etc.
2. Ask one pair to read their list out loud and write the objects on the board.
3. Ask other pairs to contribute objects that have not yet been mentioned and add these to the list. There should not be more than twelve objects on the list. If more are contributed, ask the class to vote which ones to leave out.
4. Tell the students to imagine they are incredibly wealthy. Their job is to decide which of the objects listed they would purchase, how much of their monthly income they would be willing to spend on each item and whether the purchase would be for themselves or someone else. Each student works alone with their own list.
5. Ask the students to look over their lists and decide which are their three most interesting purchases.
6. In groups of three, the students tell each other about these interesting purchases.
7. Tell them that they are about to read an article/story that deals with money. Disclose one or two details from the text, then ask the students to predict the content.

## APPLIANCES

## 3.7

**MATERIALS**
None

**LEVEL**
Intermediate +

**SKILLS**
Explaining;
Listening

**TIME**
10 minutes

**SUGGESTED TEXTS**
Any dealing with appliances, practical technology or machines

Technology has changed our lives beyond recognition and will no doubt continue to do so. People who are old enough to have experienced the advent of numerous new appliances both appreciate and somewhat dislike them. Youngsters, on the other hand, take our technology-assisted living for granted. *Appliances*, as an introductory activity, has considerably livened up some duller articles about machinery and equipment which I have, over the years, had to read with technical and ESP classes. It has also heightened my younger students' appreciation of mechanical helpers.

### Procedure

1 Ask the students to make a list of all the appliances, machines and technical equipment they use on a daily basis (telephone, washing machine, bicycle, motorbike, clothes-dryer, hairdryer, etc.).
2 While they are doing this, write the following on the board:

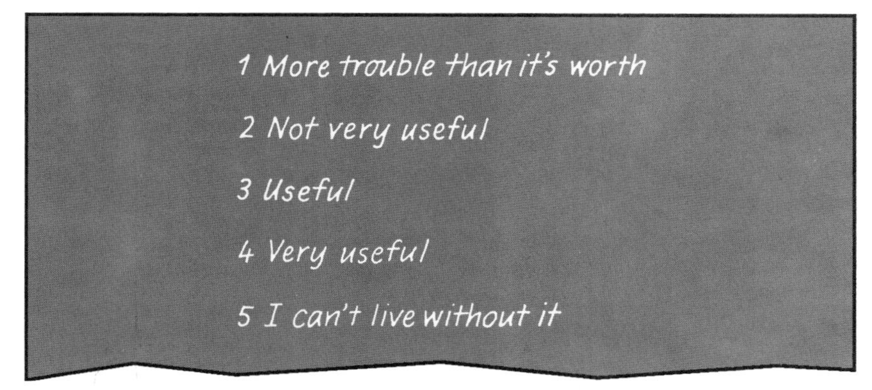


Fig. 2

3 Ask the students to mark each machine on their list 1–5 according to the chart of values written on the board. Tell them that they must have a specific reason in mind why they can't live without their motorbike or why they find a dishwasher more trouble than it's worth.
4 In groups of three, students compare and discuss their ratings of the machines.
5 In plenary, ask if anyone has heard anything of interest or anything that surprised them. If there are positive reponses to this, such as, 'I was surprised to learn that Joanna always rides a bicycle to school', ask the student to explain in more detail to the whole class. Students do not report their own views, but those of someone else in the group.
6 Tell them that they are about to read a text which deals with technical equipment and ask them to watch out for the uses of such equipment. You might wish to follow the reading with a discussion about how our lives have changed as a result of technology.

## 3.8

**MATERIALS**
An object which you yourself lost and then found again.

**LEVEL**
Intermediate +

**SKILLS**
Describing; Speaking; Listening; Asking questions

**TIME**
15–20 minutes

**SUGGESTED TEXTS**
Any text dealing with coincidences, fate or destiny

# LOST AND FOUND

This activity helps students tap in to texts which deal with the unreal, the supernatural, luck, fate and destiny. I begin this activity by showing the class an old leather wallet which I once lost and which was returned to me a year later by a librarian. All the documents which I had left in the wallet were still there, so was the money. The wallet was found by Iris, the librarian, behind a large text in the law library. Since I have never set foot in the law library, the whole thing is decidedly mysterious. The wallet contained one very precious and important letter. The letter was still in it when found. I ask my students to guess at what might have happened.

## Preparation

Look for an interesting 'lost and found' object to bring to the lesson.

## Procedure

1 Show the class your object and tell its story, or tell the story of my wallet.
2 Pair up the students so that they are facing each other. Their task is to tell each other a story of an object they once lost and later found again. If they do not have such a story, they can simply talk about an object they once lost and how they felt about this.
3 Ask if anyone has heard a particularly interesting story from their partner. If someone has, they retell it to the whole class. No one must report their own story, but rather the story they were told. Should the reporting student make mistakes in retelling, the original teller of the story can always correct.
4 Point out any coincidences or unusual occurrences in the lost and found stories and elicit more reactions to such coincidences.
5 Tell the class that you will now read a text about unusual events and ask them to look out for these as they read.

# THE TOY CAR

## 3.9

**MATERIALS**
A small toy car

**LEVEL**
Intermediate +

**SKILLS**
Speaking; Listening

**TIME**
10–15 minutes

**SUGGESTED TEXTS**
Any text dealing with road safety and/or traffic accidents

The car is an inseparable part of modern life – as are traffic accidents. EFL texts frequently include articles on road safety, accidents and transportation. *The toy car* taps memories of how toys and games influence the developing personalities of children and affect their future attitude to driving.

## Preparation

Borrow a toy car from a child of your acquaintance and bring it to the lesson.

## Procedure

1 Show the toy car to your class. Tell them that a small friend of yours left it at your house. Ask students if they also used to play with toy cars when they were small. Ask them why children enjoy playing with cars. Ask, 'How do toys and games educate children for their future adult roles?' Allow students to write down some notes in answer to these questions.
2 Arrange your class into groups of three and ask them to pool their answers.
3 Regroup the class into new groups of three. Ask them to discuss how one can educate children to become better and more careful drivers in the future.
4 Tell them that they are going to read a text on road safety and ask them to look out for any hints about education for responsible driving.

## 3.10

**MATERIALS**
A packet of cigarettes

**LEVEL**
Intermediate +

**SKILLS**
Speaking; Listening

**TIME**
10–15 minutes

**SUGGESTED TEXTS**
Any text which deals with smoking or addictions

# CIGARETTE PACKET

There is now proof beyond a shadow of a doubt that cigarette smoking causes dreadful diseases including cancer. In the EFL class, we often study texts related to smoking or various other drug addictions. *Cigarette packet* is a useful introduction to such texts.

## Procedure

1 Hold up the cigarette packet and ask students how the wrapping serves as an advertisement for the product. Accept all responses.
2 Ask, 'Does anyone know of anything on this packet that opposes the sale of the product?' Someone in the class will probably know about the Government Health Warning. If not, point it out to the class. Ask a student to read it out loud. American packets read 'The Surgeon General Warns That Cigarette Smoking Is Dangerous To Your Health', while British cigarettes have a range of warnings, such as 'Warning: Smoking Can Cause Heart Disease', or 'Smoking Can Seriously Damage Your Health'. Ask the students if they think that such warnings stop people from smoking.
3 In pairs or groups ask students to make a list of steps that a school or a society might take to combat smoking or drug abuse.
4 In plenary, elicit one group's list. Write it on the board. Then ask the other groups to contribute any missing items.
5 Tell them that they will read a text about the problem and ask them to be on the lookout for items similar to those they have already mentioned.

# CHAPTER 4

# *Words, words, and a bit more than words*

## *Making use of key vocabulary*

One word can suggest endless associations. A good word and we become someone's willing slave – a harsh word and some of us crumble.

In the language classroom these volatile items are just tools of the trade. Sometimes we forget that they are charged with meaning. We treat them perfunctorily and sap their potency. This chapter shows how to recharge them a bit!

## THIS MAKES ME THINK OF THAT

**4.1**

**MATERIALS**
None

**LEVEL**
Intermediate +

**SKILLS**
Speaking; Guessing and predicting; Asking questions; Using modals

**TIME**
15–20 minutes

**SUGGESTED TEXTS**
Poems, prose selections or articles

Although we are not always aware of it, we all think poetically. That is, when something stimulates our thinking we make associations – both concrete and abstract. This activity is for introducing a text by triggering such poetic thinking.

### Preparation

Look through your text and choose one word which is either central to, or evocative of, the gist of the text. In the text below, 'Hope is the Thing with Feathers', I have chosen the word *bird* to serve the purpose, but any single word will do, though, as a rule, nouns work best.

Hope is the Thing with Feathers

Hope is the thing with feathers –
That perches in the soul –
And sings the tune without the words –
And never stops – at all –

And sweetest – in the Gale – is heard –
And sore must be the storm –
That could abash the little Bird –
That kept so many warm –

I've heard it in the chillest land –
And on the strangest Sea –
Yet never, in Extremity,
It asked a crumb – of me.

Johnson, T.H. *The Complete Poems of Emily Dickinson* Little Brown and Co. 1960 p.254

## Procedure

1 Tell the students the word you have chosen and ask them to think of as many associations as possible that come to their minds when they hear this word. Give them one to two minutes.

2 Pair the students up and ask them to compare their lists and brainstorm together for additional items. Allow three to five minutes for this.

3 Ask the students to call out the words on their lists and, as they do so write them on the board in two columns. One column should include abstract words, the other concrete ones. The word, *bird*, for example, has yielded concrete words such as *cage, wings, feathers, seed, worms, nest,* and abstract words such as *freedom, liberty, lightness, air, escape.*

4 If you would rather not do all this writing on the board, ask two students, one in charge of each column, to do it. Your job then is simply to tell them which side the word belongs on.

5 Ask the class why there are two columns. If no one can explain, do so yourself, stressing that we all think in both concrete and abstract terms.

6 Ask the students to predict what the text will be about. They must answer without using the key word. In the above example, using *bird*, the sample predictions were, 'The text might be about someone who escapes.' 'It might be about freedom.' 'It could be about animals that fly.'

7 Ask the students to write five questions about the imagined text. They may do this in pairs. Sample questions for this text might be, Why does the writer write about birds? What kind of birds are they? Is this a text for entertainment or education? When was the text written? How does the writer feel about birds?

8 Ask them to read out their questions. Answer them and then ask whether they have changed their minds about the probable content of the text.

**VARIATIONS**

i For a less capable group, instead of having students make their own associations, hand out a list of suggested associations and ask them to make choices from this list. In the question-making sessions, questions can be prompted with starters such as 'Why does?', 'How long?', 'What kind?', etc.

ii With more able students, ask one student to preread the text and answer the class's questions in Step 8.

# WHOLESOME SCATTERING

I am sometimes surprised to see how evocative single words can be. When I use this activity, students, on occasion not only predict the content of the passage they are about to read, but also almost duplicate sentences which actually appear in it. If you have a creative class, you might find that the first step of arranging the words in weird and unusual ways is fun and takes quite a while. I think it is worth the effort. These are words students will not quickly forget!

## Preparation

Choose twelve to sixteen key words from the text you are going to read with your class.

## Procedure

1 Ask three to five students to come to the board. Their task is to write down words you dictate. (In a good class, ask a student to dictate.) Each student writes each word so that each word is written as many times as there are students at the board. They scatter these words at random all over the board, and try to arrange the words in unusual ways. Some will be written horizontally, other vertically, others in shapes, others upside down. Do not comment on spelling at this stage. Some students will change their spelling as they observe how the student next to them has spelt a word or as they are corrected by others in the class.

2 While the students at the board are doing this, those in their seats can produce their own arrangements of the words either on paper or in their notebooks.

3 When you have finished dictating the words, the students who were at the board return to their seats.

4 Ask if anyone in the class thinks they have produced a particularly unusual arrangement of the words. If there are volunteers, ask them to display their arrangements.

5 Go over the words on the board, eliciting correct spelling and meaning.

6 Ask the students, in pairs, to write as many sentences as possible using the words on the board. They should try to put more than one of the words in each sentence. Tell them that they have only three minutes for this.

7 Stop them when the time is up and ask pairs to tell you how many sentences they have succeeded in writing.

8 Ask each pair to read out its best sentence.

9 Ask the class to predict the content of the text they are about to read.

**4.2**

**MATERIALS**
None

**LEVEL**
Elementary +

**SKILLS**
Writing sentences; Predicting

**TIME**
10–15 minutes

**SUGGESTED TEXTS**
Any text

## 4.3

**MATERIALS**
None

**LEVEL**
Intermediate +

**SKILLS**
Categorising;
Predicting

**TIME**
10–15 minutes

**SUGGESTED TEXTS**
Any text

# HOT OR COLD

We learn best that with which we have an emotional connection. *Hot or cold* asks students to give emotional value to a word. Interestingly, I have found that students who are not willing to share themselves on an emotional level are quite able to participate in this activity in a most concrete and cognitive manner. I always remember a very scientifically–minded young woman who labelled the word *frustration* 'cold' because, 'I always get so frustrated when I try to get the ice-cubes out of the fridge.'

## Preparation

Choose ten to fifteen key words from the text you are going to read. Put the words on the board before the lesson or photocopy the list for each student.

## Procedure

**1** Write this at the top of the board:

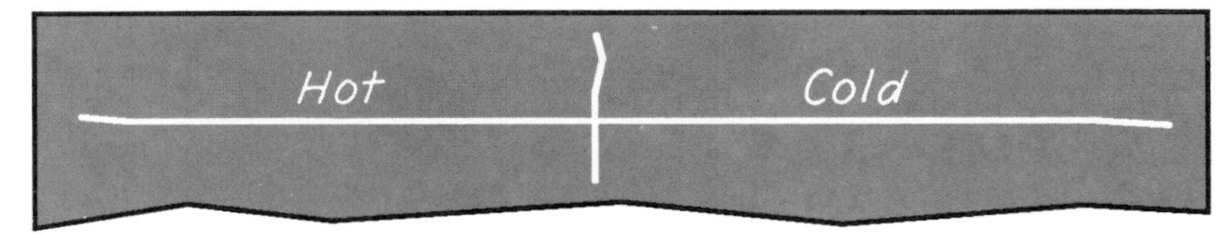


Fig. 3

and ask students to copy it.

**2** Elicit the meanings of the words on the list. Supply them yourself when students are unable to give the meaning. Using dictionaries is not advisable here as it would be too time-consuming.

**3** Ask the students to write the words either in the 'Hot' or in the 'Cold' column. Words they are not sure about go in the middle. Tell them that before they place a word somewhere it should be quite clear to them why they are doing so. Stress that their reasons for putting words where they do are strictly personal and individual and have nothing to do with where other students might place their words. For example, from the following list, *contain, subtract, consent, register, failure, palm, porch,* my student Yoko put *porch* in the middle, because 'We sit on the porch when the weather is nice – not too hot or too cold.' She put *consent* under cold because 'I feel cold and terrible every time I consent to do what my mother wants me to'. She put *register* under hot because she was 'hot and excited' about a course in dancing she had just registered for.

**4** Put students into groups of three or four and ask them to tell each other where they put their words and why.

**5** Write the first or last sentence of the text on the board. Ask them to consider this sentence and the list of words they have just studied and ask them to predict the content of the text they are going to read.

# WATER, WATER EVERYWHERE

**4.4**

**MATERIALS**
Copies of a list of words from the text

**LEVEL**
Intermediate +

**SKILLS**
Categorising; Predicting

**TIME**
15–20 minutes

**SUGGESTED TEXTS**
Any text

Here is a way of leading into a text by using well-known vocabulary to introduce less-known vocabulary. Weaker students enjoy the activity because they can usually become chief contributors to its opening stages.

## Preparation

Choose ten to fifteen key words from the text you are going to read. Write them on the board before the lesson or prepare a photocopy for each student.

## Procedure

1 Elicit or explain the meanings of the words.
2 Ask students to sit in pairs and together make another vocabulary list. This list is to consist of any words they can think of that are connected to *water*. This may be anything from *ocean* to *tap*. Tell them to work fast as they are only allowed two minutes for this activity.
3 Ask one pair for their list and write it on the board.
4 Ask other pairs to contribute anything they feel this pair left out. Your final list might look something like this:

| | |
|---|---|
| *stream* | *rain* |
| *river* | *beach* |
| *lake* | *fountain* |
| *tears* | *waterfall* |
| *bath* | *brook* |
| *bucket* | *shower* |

5 Ask the students to form associations between any water word and a word from the original list you gave them. If your original list contained the words:

| | |
|---|---|
| *blacksmith* | *narrowminded* |
| *location* | *despair* |
| *struggle* | |

a student might put *blacksmith* with *shower*, because a blacksmith certainly needs to shower after a day's work. They might put *narrowminded* with *tears*, because narrowminded people upset them to tears. Students should be told that their associations are strictly individual and personal and have nothing to do with what other students have done.
6 Tell students approximately where in the text to be read (beginning, middle or end) the words you have studied fit, and ask them to predict the content of the text.

## 4.5 CHAIN REACTION

**MATERIALS**
None

**LEVEL**
Elementary +

**SKILLS**
Predicting; Making up sentences

**TIME**
10–15 minutes

**SUGGESTED TEXTS**
Any text

This is another activity which uses word associations to sensitise learners to the topic of the text.

### Procedure

1 Divide the class into groups. (See Note below.) Ask each group to form a semicircle. Designate the student at each end of each semicircle as 'first' or 'last'.
2 For each group appoint a secretary who will not otherwise participate but will be responsible for writing all words called out. The secretary is not to write the associative, or explanatory sentences, only the words.
3 Write the first and the last noun from the text on the board.
4 The 'first' student in each group is responsible for the first word and the 'last' student for the last word. The first student says the first noun and then another word (it need not be a noun) that the first word triggered in their associative imagination. Next, the student gives a sentence explaining the association. For example, if the first noun is *bread*, the first student might then say, *eat*. 'That makes me think of eat because I love eating bread'.
5 The second student must instantly react to that association. 'That makes me think of *hungry* because it is almost time to eat and I really feel hungry.' And so on.
6 The tricky part falls to the last student in the semicircle who must link the word they receive from the previous student to the last noun of the text. Most students are up to the challenge.
7 The secretary for each group reads out all the word associations they have recorded. This is particularly interesting in large classes where each group has made a different set of associations.

**NOTE**
For this activity to work well you need to keep up a brisk pace. Students who can't think of what to say when their turn comes must pass. If several students in a row are stuck and pass, give a response yourself or ask for help from other students. In a small class (under twenty students) the entire class can participate. In medium-sized classes (twenty to thirty-five students), divide the class into two or three groups. In very large classes (over thirty-five) divide the class into groups of seven to eight students each.

## THOUGHTS AND FEELINGS

**4.6**

**MATERIALS**
None

**LEVEL**
Intermediate +

**SKILLS**
Categorising; Dictation

**TIME**
15–20 minutes

**SUGGESTED TEXTS**
Articles or essays expressing a strong point of view

We have all felt insulted by a word or two said in the wrong way at the wrong moment while a word of encouragement at the right time can turn our whole world right again. Somehow we are not always aware of the power of words in a foreign language. This is an activity that sharpens that awareness.

### Preparation

Choose ten or twelve key words from the text and write them on the board before the lesson starts.

### Procedure

1 Ask each student to divide a piece of paper into three columns and head one column with the word 'Thoughts', another with 'Feelings' and the third column with 'Not certain.'
2 Dictate the following statements to your class or ask a student who reads well to dictate them. As the sentences are dictated, students write them under one of the three headings.

- I never cry in public.
- She laughs when people make mistakes.
- Think before you speak!
- He makes a list of everything he has to do every day.
- She always checks her maths problems carefully.

3 Ask the students to sit in small groups and explain to each other which heading they placed each sentence under. For example, one student might write the first sentence under 'Emotions' because people cry when they are sad and sadness is an emotion. Another student might put in under 'Thoughts', saying 'This is true for me because it's important what other people think of me'.
4 Tell them that just as they disagreed on sentences they would probably disagree on where words belonged, since words too carry overtones of emotion. Ask them to look at the list of words you have written on the board, and elicit or explain their meanings.
5 Ask the students to write each word in one of the three columns.
6 In pairs, students explain their categorisation to each other.
7 Tell them that the text they are about to read also deals with both thoughts and feelings. Tell them to be on the lookout for this as they read.

ACKNOWLEDGEMENT
This activity is a variation of one that I learned in a workshop with Mario Rinvolucri during the 1987 IATEFL conference in Edinburgh, Scotland.

## 4.7

**MATERIALS**
None

**LEVEL**
Intermediate +

**SKILLS**
Categorising;
Explaining;
Predicting

**TIME**
10–15 minutes

**SUGGESTED TEXTS**
Any text

# THE RAINBOW

*The rainbow* allows students to react affectively towards words as they mentally colour them in all the shades of the rainbow. The activity is particularly interesting in multilingual, multicultural classes since colours represent different moods and attitudes in different cultures. An African student told me that in his country the colour blue symbolises youth, while in America this is the colour of sadness and in other countries it is thought to guard against the evil eye. White is the symbol of purity to some and mourning to others. Red reflects passion and anger to some and vitality to others. Green stands for life in some cultures while in others it symbolises inexperience or envy. Yellow can be cowardice, wealth or jealousy depending on where on the globe you are. All of this creates lively group discussion in the EFL classroom.

## Preparation

Choose twelve to fifteen key words from the text you are going to read and write them up on one side of the board before the lesson.

## Procedure

1 Pair up students and ask them to work together to make a list of as many colours as they can think of.
2 Ask one pair to read out their list. Pick a pair who, as a rule, do not contribute much. This time, since they are dealing with elementary vocabulary, they should have a nice size list. Write their contributions on the free side of the board.
3 Ask other pairs to add colours not mentioned by the first pair. Add these to the list.
4 Draw the attention of the class to the original vocabulary list you have written on the board. Elicit or explain the meanings of the words.
5 Ask the students to give each word a colour and to be able to explain why they have chosen that particular colour for the word. Remind them that their choices of colour are strictly personal, depend on their own impressions and have nothing to do with the way other students decide to colour words.
6 Put the students in small groups and ask them to explain to each other how and why they have coloured their words.
7 Tell them that these are key words from the text they are about to read and elicit predictions about the content of the text.

# WORDS ON MY WAY

## 4.8

**MATERIALS**
None

**LEVEL**
Intermediate +

**SKILLS**
Categorising; Explaining; Scanning

**TIME**
15–20 minutes

**SUGGESTED TEXTS**
Any text dealing with places and/or travel

This activity eases students into a text by placing key words into a familiar scene. It worked particularly well once when I had a class in which many of my students who lived in the same neighbourhood discovered, much to their own amazement, that they were putting words into completely different places. The same thing happened in a university EFL class where many of the students lived in the same dormitory on campus. The fact that they all placed words from the same list in entirely different locations on the same piece of road highlighted not only their individuality, but by being so individual to them, also facilitated their recollection of the words in question.

## Preparation

Choose eight to fifteen key words from the text and write these on the board before the lesson starts.

## Procedure

1 Ask the students to draw a map of the route they take from their home to the school. Ask them to put in street names, names of shops they pass, important buildings and significant trees or billboards. It should be strictly a memory map so it need not be terribly accurate. If two or more students come from the same place, let them help each other out, but don't dwell too long on this. The whole thing should not take more than about three minutes.
2 Ask students to read the list of vocabulary items you put on the board. Elicit and/or explain the meanings.
3 Ask the students to place each word somewhere on their personal map. They must make sure that they know why they are placing each word in its place. For example, 'I put the word *desire* over the sweet shop I pass, because I feel a strong desire to buy some chocolate' or 'I put *struggle* over that large tree because I once saw a cat who did not want a struggle with a dog climb up there.'

   On page 46 is a typical vocabulary list and how such a list might look on a student map.
4 Ask students, in groups of three, to explain to each other where they placed each word and why they put it there.
5 Tell them that they are going to read a text which also deals with places. Tell them to be on the lookout for the words they have been working with as they read the text.

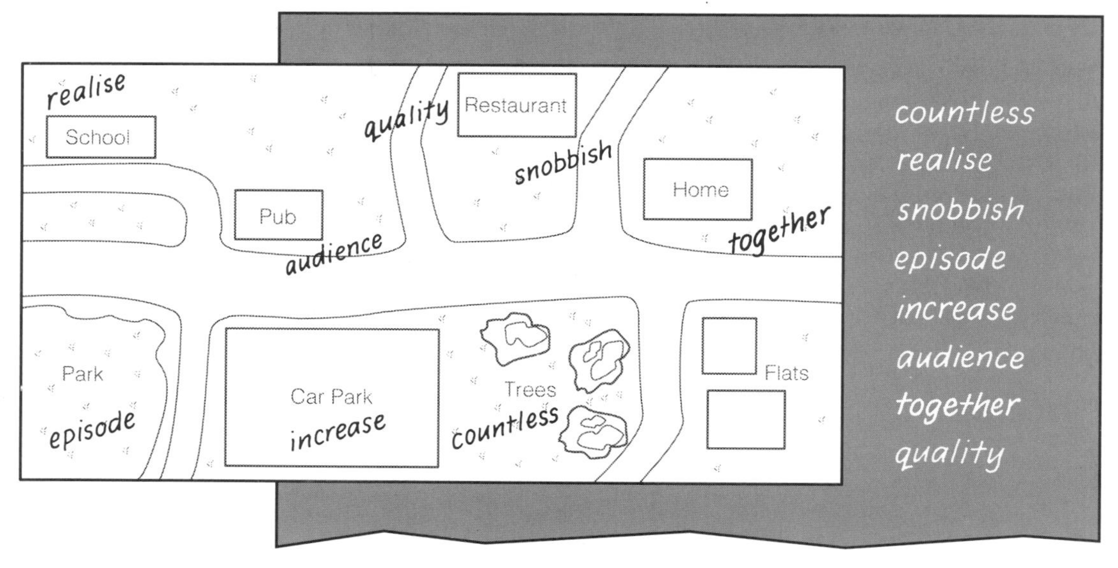


Fig. 4

## 4.9

**MATERIALS**
None

**LEVEL**
Intermediate +

**SKILLS**
Writing; Predicting

**TIME**
20–25 minutes with Steps 4 and 5.
10–15 minutes without Steps 4 and 5.

**SUGGESTED TEXTS**
Advertisements

# ADVERTISING WORDS

Here we approach a text 'upside down'. That is, by giving content first and then asking for vocabulary afterwards.

## Procedure

1 Divide the class into small groups. Their task will be to think about how one might advertise a product one wants to sell. The product can be anything that the text you are planning to read advertises. You may wish to ask all the groups to consider the same product or if your text(s) deal(s) with many products, assign one product to each group. For example, Group A may deal with cosmetics, Group B with cakes, Group C with wines, etc.

2 Each group appoints a secretary. They then brainstorm words they could use to advertise their product while the secretary jots them down. For example, if a group was assigned facial cream as its product, the students might come up with words and phrases such as *smooth, silky, easy to apply, makes you beautiful, soft, youthful,* etc. Allow three to five minutes for this.

3 The secretary of each group tells the whole class what their product was and which words they have listed. Members of the class may suggest other vocabulary. All the vocabulary is recorded on the board either by you or by a student assigned to the job. This is especially interesting if all the groups have been dealing with one product, as the vocabulary often does not overlap.

The next three steps may be omitted, but they work well with more able groups.

4 Using the vocabulary on the board, the students, in small groups, compose advertisements for their products.
5 The groups read their advertisements out loud.
6 Tell the class that they will read real advertisements that sell their products. Ask them to look out for 'their' vocabulary.

ACKNOWLEDGEMENT
This is a variation of a technique I learned from Carol Golfus of the Israeli Ministry of Education when she lectured to a group of immigrant teachers.

## SHOUT IT OUT

**4.10**

**MATERIALS**
None

**LEVEL**
Beginner +

**SKILLS**
Skimming

**TIME**
10–20 minutes

**SUGGESTED TEXTS**
Any text

This activity is an energy releaser, suitable for classes that like hamming it up a bit! Actually, I have found that reticent students are willing to participate in this activity since the speaking and acting is choral.

### Preparation

Choose ten to twelve key words from the text to be read and write them on the board before the lesson.

### Procedure

1 Tell the class that they are going to read a text in which the words on the board appear.
2 Elicit and/or explain the meanings of the words.
3 Divide the class into small groups. Tell each group that they must choose one word only and act it out with a shout. They must use gestures that will help explain the meaning of the word. The shouting out and the movements must be done by the whole group together. For example, the whole group might say the word *despair* in a low, sad voice while they are all stretching their arms upwards in supplication and making facial expressions of great sadness.
4 Allow them three to five minutes to choose the word and decide on the action. During this time the group may go outside and practice.
5 At a prearranged time, all the groups enter the room and each group in turn performs to (teacher encouraged?) applause. The rest of the class guesses which word they are performing.
6 Remind the students that they will be reading a passage in which the 'acted-out' words appear, and tell them to be on the lookout for these.

# CHAPTER 5

# *Write it right*

## *Using written activities*

Many of us find writing difficult. Writing is hard work, writing means rewriting, writing is red marks – work for the teacher and a put-down for the student. Writing is communicating to someone who, at best, answers much later and maybe not at all.

In this chapter, as we use written activities to introduce texts, we will try to make our writing more pleasant and less threatening.

## 5.1 THE OUTRAGED LETTER

**MATERIALS**
One 'outraged letter' for each small group

**LEVEL**
Advanced

**SKILLS**
Writing; Discussion; Reading

**TIME**
20–30 minutes

**SUGGESTED TEXTS**
Articles dealing with controversial subjects

This activity is excellent when introducing a text dealing with a controversial issue. However, any topic can, with a little imagination, be turned into a controversial issue.

### Preparation

Write a letter in which you play the devil's advocate. Be strongly for or strongly against the issue to be discussed in your text. Address your letter to some person or group plausibly connected to your issue. This could be the editor of a newspaper, the head of a school, a politician or any interested party. For example, I used the outraged letter on page 49 to introduce a poetry unit. Such a letter can, of course, be written on almost any subject.

### Procedure

1 Divide the class into small groups, each a group of experts. Their task is to discuss and answer the outraged letter. The last time students answered my 'angry father letter' they became the teachers and the head of an English department. They may become groups of psychologists, groups of journalists, doctors, social workers or whatever fits the subject of your letter. Clothing students in a mantle of expertise in this way invariably produces interesting results.

2 If you have a very good class, you may now wish to assign students special roles within the group. There may be one person who basically agrees with the message of the letter, one who strongly disagrees, one who is not sure, one who disagrees but feels that one must be very diplomatic, one who feels very angry and wants to tell

the writer off. Give your group about ten minutes to discuss this letter and to attempt to reach a consensus. If roles have been assigned, students should talk from the position of their role.

**3** The students compose an answer to the letter, one per group. Give ten to fifteen minutes for this task.

**4** In plenary, listen to several letters. If your class is small, listen to all of them. If it is large, hear one or two additional suggestions from groups which do not usually read their letters.

**5** Make a bridge sentence to the text, such as 'We have heard a great deal said about ________. Let's take a look at what our text says about it.'

To the head of the English Department.

Dear Sir or Madam,

I was terribly upset and unhappy to learn that my son Peter has to study poetry in his English class. What a ridiculous idea! You people really don't know what you are doing! Poetry is hard enough to read in a person's native language, and completely out of the question in a foreign language!

English is one of the most important subjects studied in school. What a shame to waste lessons in this way. We are a technically minded family. We strongly feel that Peter and his friends should study technical articles and news articles in English classes so as to better prepare themselves for life.

Leave the poetry to the poets!

Yours faithfully

An angry and upset father

Fig. 5

ACKNOWLEDGEMENT

This is a variation of a technique I learned in a workshop given by Penny Ur, author of *Discussions That Work: Task-centred Fluency Practice* (CUP 1981).

## 5.2

**MATERIALS**
None

**LEVEL**
Advanced

**SKILLS**
Discussion; Writing

**TIME**
15–20 minutes

**SUGGESTED TEXTS**
Any text dealing with social injustice

# UPSIDE DOWN OUTRAGE

This activity works well with teenage students. At this problematic age, students are often dissatisfied and angry at those whom they see as authority figures. This activity enables you to channel such dissatisfaction productively.

If you feel stirrings of anger in the class directed against an unfair test, a new school policy or an allegedly unfair assignment, capture these in the *Upside down outrage*. I have found that even when the outrage was directed against one of my own policies, the tension was considerably alleviated through a fairly lighthearted use of *Outrage*. The activity can, of course, also be used as a forum for outcry against any social injustice. I recommend it as a prereading activity to an article or story which deals with social problems.

## Procedure

1. Write the central issue of your text on the board. For example, 'Homelessness', 'Unfair school policy', etc.
2. Pair the students up and ask them to tell each other what they know about the issue and how they feel about it.
3. Let the whole class hear reports from several pairs. Note salient points on the board.
4. Ask each pair to 'adopt' another pair. The task of these foursomes is to compose an outraged letter about the issue. They may address the letter to any person in authority who is somehow connected with the problem, such as a head of a school, the mayor of a city, the editor of a newspaper, etc.
5. In plenary, ask several students to read their letters out loud.
6. Tell the class that expressing social attitudes, as they have done, is important and that they are about to read an article on the same (or another) controversial issue. Ask them to be on the lookout for the point of view of the writer.

## TAKE A STAND

## 5.3

**MATERIALS**
None

**LEVEL**
Advanced

**SKILLS**
Writing;
Discussion;
Dictation

**TIME**
10 minutes

**SUGGESTED TEXTS**
Texts concerned with serious issues

This activity asks students to write a 'one minute paper' on any issue of concern. Being forced to write very quickly is an effective way to remove writer's block. In addition, I have used one minute papers to practise fluency in writing as well as to introduce texts. This fluency is the kind of free outpouring that does not bother with such writing nicities as spelling, punctuation or even details of meaning.

### Procedure

1. Tell the students that you are going to dictate the beginning of a sentence to them and that they are to continue writing where you leave off. They can finish the sentence and start as many new sentences as they have time for but what they are writing should hang together and be the continuation of the first idea. They write until you tell them to stop. Tell them that they are not to worry about spelling or getting exactly the right word but to simply let their thoughts flow and their pens move. If they can't think of the right word in English, they may either leave a blank, ask you, or use the counterpart in their native language – whatever is the easiest for them and does not break their train of thought.
2. Dictate to them, 'When I consider *old age*, (or whatever issue your reading text deals with) I often wonder...'
3. Signal the students to continue writing.
4. Allow them to write for one or two minutes then ask them to stop.
5. Ask the students to sit in groups of three and share their written thoughts. It is better that they do not read them out, but rather talk about what they have written.
6. Tell them that they will now read a text that deals with the same issue.

## 5.4

**MATERIALS**
None

**LEVEL**
Elementary +

**SKILLS**
Dictation;
Skimming

**TIME**
10–15 minutes

**SUGGESTED TEXTS**
Any text

# CRYPTIC DICTATION

This is basically a skimming activity. I have found it soothing for it does not involve much thinking or creativity and is fine for the student who likes serious and fairly challenging work.

## Preparation

Choose a short paragraph from a text which you plan to read in great detail with your class. Change a few crucial details in the paragraph. Change a place name, or make a tall, thin person round and fat or make a house a flat, or change a few adverbs into their opposites. You should not make more than five changes.

## Procedure

1. Dictate the changed paragraph to your class.
2. Ask several students to read the paragraph out loud.
3. Tell them that you have taken this paragraph from the text that you will soon be reading, but that you have made some changes.
4. Ask them to guess at the changes. Accept all guesses.
5. Ask students to work in pairs, skimming the text until they find the paragraph and are able to 'correct' the changes.

## 5.5

**MATERIALS**
None

**LEVEL**
Elementary +

**SKILLS**
Note-taking;
Lecturing;
Dictation; Asking and answering questions

**TIME**
15–20 minutes

**SUGGESTED TEXTS**
Texts whose primary purpose is to inform or educate

# MINI LECTURE

*Mini lecture* is good for stimulating that student whose oral abilities are above the level of the class and who likes to shine. It is also a useful technique for very structured pair work, especially with scientifically-minded students.

## Preparation

1. Appoint a capable student to summarise the essay or article you are going to read with your class. Give this student a copy of the text to read.
2. Tell this student that their task will be to deliver a five minute lecture in which they summarise the main ideas of the article.
3. Prepare four questions on the article. Before the lesson check with the student, making sure that their 'mini lecture' contains the answers to your questions.

## Procedure

1. Give your list of questions to a student who reads well. This student doesn't need them now but keeps them for later.

2 Divide your class in two by making alternate students say the word *in* or *out*. As they do so, tell them to remember who they are – 'ins' or 'outs'.
3 Ask the 'outs' to go outside the classroom, together with the student to whom you have given your list of questions. (See Step 1.) Ask them to take pens and paper with them.
4 Outside the classroom the student with the questions dictates them to the others.
5 Meanwhile, the student who has prepared the mini lecture delivers it to the students remaining in the classroom.
6 The 'out' students are invited back in.
7 Each 'out' pairs up with an 'in' and asks the dictated questions. The 'ins' answer, possibly checking their notes as they do so.
8 The whole class reviews the information by going over the questions and noting the varieties of answers.

ACKNOWLEDGEMENT
This activity incorporates a variation of a technique I learned from Kevin Keating at the Center of English as a Second Language at the University of Arizona, Tucson, Arizona.

## BRANCHING OUT

**5.6**

**MATERIALS**
None

**LEVEL**
Intermediate +

**SKILLS**
Writing; Sentence completion; Explaining

**TIME**
10–15 minutes

**SUGGESTED TEXTS**
Any text

This is a sentence completion activity that permits creativity and flexibility within a framework. The writing here is minimal, since first only the secretary of the group writes and later a group representative writes on the board. This activity prepares students well for writing a text summary, so you might wish to set one for homework.

### Preparation

Read through the text and write one stem sentence for each small group in the class. The stem sentences should reveal some of the content of your text, but it should be possible to finish them in many different ways. An example of a stem sentence might be, *People who live in New York love their city because...*

### Procedure

1 Tell the class that they will be reading a text about a particular subject and that you want them to think about it.
2 Divide the class into small groups and ask each group to appoint a secretary.
3 Give each group one stem sentence and ask them to finish it in as many ways as they can in three minutes. All group members contribute ideas and the secretary records them.

4 Ask the groups to call out the number of sentences they succeeded in making. Praise high achievers and ask the 'winning' group to read out their sentences. With each sentence, the original stem sentence must be repeated. For example:
*The people of New York love their city because it is exciting.*
*The people of New York love their city because it has a great theatre.*
*The people of New York love their city because there are so many different kinds of people living in it, etc.*
5 When this group finishes its reading, encourage students from other groups to add to that particular stem if they have thought of a good sentence.
6 Ask each group to choose their best sentence and write it on the board.
7 The students read the text and compare what it says with the completed sentences on the board.

## 5.7

**MATERIALS**
None

**LEVEL**
Advanced

**SKILLS**
Describing; Writing; Discussion

**TIME**
20–25 minutes

**SUGGESTED TEXTS**
Texts dealing with archaeology, history or ancient cultures

## THE ARCHAEOLOGICAL REPORT

This works best with very creative classes. I have used it as an introduction to an essay about an archaeological dig, and also as a lead-in to Shelley's poem 'Ozymandias'.

### Procedure

1 Divide the class into small groups. Each group appoints a secretary.
2 Tell them to imagine that they are a group of archaeologists who have just dug up an ancient object.
3 Their task is to write a letter to their immediate supervisor in London (or in their own capital city) describing this extraordinary find. They must explain what the object is. They should describe its size, colour, and what it is made of. They should also speculate on the use of this object in the ancient world and what this find might tell us about the society in which it was used. They should convey their excitement about the find.
4 In plenary, the groups read out their letters.
5 Talk with the class about why people are so fascinated by ancient objects. Tell them that they will read a text that deals with the issue.

# LETTER OF RECOMMENDATION

**5.8**

**MATERIALS**
None

**LEVEL**
Advanced

**SKILLS**
Dictation;
Discussion;
Writing;
Comparing texts

**TIME**
20–25 minutes

**SUGGESTED TEXTS**
Fiction and/or non-fiction texts which deal with work, making impressions, or with prejudice or stereotypes

This is a good introductory activity for texts dealing with the world of work, as well as texts describing prejudice and stereotypical thinking. I have used it as an introduction to 'Mr Knowall,' a short story by Somerset Maugham, and an essay by John Steinbeck called, 'How to tell the Good Guys from the Bad Guys'.

## Procedure

1 Divide the class into groups of three or four. Each group appoints a secretary.
2 Tell them that they are supervisors in the ministry of culture and education in their country. An employee of the ministry, a Mr Ican Getthere, is applying for promotion and has asked them for a letter of recommendation.
3 Dictate the following information about him to your class:

- He dresses very conservatively.
- He is quiet and never starts a conversation.
- He has few friends.
- His work is always neat, but never outstanding.
- He lives with his mother.
- He is thirty-five years old and is not married.

4 Using this information, one third of the groups writes a very favourable letter about Mr Ican Getthere, one third writes a very negative letter, and the last third writes a neutral letter. The ideas should be discussed and clarified in each group before the secretary writes. Allow about ten minutes for this activity and circulate among the groups helping out with vocabulary.
5 In plenary, ask at least one group from each category (pro, con and indifferent) to read out their letter. It is interesting to note that those who write favourable letters use vocabulary such as *modest, pleasant, quiet, unassuming, chooses friends carefully, works with caution and avoids mistakes.* Those who write negative letters make Mr Getthere *snobbish, withdrawn, unsociable* and *unimaginative.* Those with neutral letters use the adjectives they were given almost unchanged.
6 If the text deals with stereotypical or prejudiced thinking, point out to the class that we often see things the way we decide they should be seen. Should your text deal with the world of work, point out how important recommendations are when you look for a new job or seek promotion. Ask them to look out for any points you have discussed in the text they will read.

ACKNOWLEDGEMENT
This activity is a variation of one I learned in a workshop by Carol Goldfus of the Israel Ministry of Education.

## 5.9

**MATERIALS**
None

**LEVEL**
Intermediate +

**SKILLS**
Writing; Asking questions

**TIME**
25–30 minutes

**SUGGESTED TEXTS**
Biographical or autobiographical writing, journal or diary writing

# DIALOGUE JOURNAL

We are all intensely interested in ourselves. Keeping this in mind can help us make the EFL class a more interesting place for our students. Writing, like every other skill, is more vibrantly experienced if the total involvement of the writer can be felt. The function of a dialogue journal is to make the events of our own daily lives interesting to someone else. This is what good writers do all the time.

*Dialogue journal* is a time-consuming activity, but if you see it as an introduction to a unit on biographical texts, I think that you will consider the time well invested. This is especially true if you repeat the activity during your progress through the biographical text.

## Procedure

1. Ask the students if they have ever kept a journal. How long did they succeed in keeping it? Was it a rewarding or frustrating experience? What was difficult about it?
2. Tell the students that two things are reported to be difficult for journal writers. One is the feeling that what they wrote was basically boring and that they themselves are not even interested in reading it. The other is the feeling that one is writing into a kind of void. This is a frustrating feeling because writing, just like speaking, is a communicative activity. In other words, when we write, we want to reach someone, even if that person is an older other-self. (If you manage to elicit these points in Step 1, omit Step 2.)
3. Tell the students that they are about to have a chance to tell someone else, in the most interesting way possible, about an event in their lives. Their writing will be read and reacted to and they, in turn, will react to someone else's writing.
4. Pair them up and ask them to sit facing each other. Tell them that the person sitting opposite them is their writing partner.
5. Tell them that you will give them the opening sentence and that they are to continue writing until you stop them. Their task is to write about something they did or something that happened to them. However, they must start right inside the event, because they will not have much time to write. In other words, if they want to write about how a woman in the supermarket pushed them, they should start with the woman and not with how they had to go to the supermarket that morning.
6. Dictate the sentence 'I really must tell you about...' Signal everyone to start writing.
7. Circulate while they write, helping out with vocabulary.
8. Stop them after about seven minutes.
9. Ask them to swap journals with their partners.
10. Their task now is to read their partner's journal and respond in the following manner. Write these items on the board.

a **Say at least one positive thing about your partner's journal.** This must be something specific. They should not say anything as general as, 'I really liked what you wrote'. However, they could say, 'I really liked what you wrote because I have been in such a situation myself' or, 'You really made me see that woman..', etc.
b **Ask one or two questions about the journal.**
c **Try to relate your partner's journal to your own experience.** If they can't do this, they should explain why not.
d **Write anything else that comes to mind as you read your partner's journal.**
Allow about seven minutes for this writing activity.

11 Ask the students to return the journals to their partners and give them a few minutes to read what their partner has written.
12 Tell them that you will spend some time reading a text which is (or is like) a personal history written down in a journal.

## CARD GAME

## 5.10

**MATERIALS**
Index cards (at least one for each student in your class)

**LEVEL**
Intermediate +

**SKILLS**
Writing; Summarising

**TIME**
15–20 minutes

**SUGGESTED TEXTS**
Any informative text

This provides an opportunity to write concisely and share information. It is a good activity for a bright, rather scientifically-minded class in which students take pride in how much general knowledge they have. It has worked very well for me with a class of Japanese engineers.

### Procedure

1 Give each student an index card.
2 Tell the students that they will be reading a text about ______.
3 Ask them to summarise, in note form, all they think that they know about this topic. Their summary must not exceed fifty words and must fit on the index card. Give them three to five minutes for this activity.
4 Collect all the index cards and arrange them in a fan as you would for a card game.
5 Walk around the class and ask the students to pull out one card each. If they pull out their own, they should put it back and pull out another.
6 Ask them to read their card and try to find any information that they either did not know or for some reason did not put on their own card.
7 Ask the students to sit in groups of four and share any information they have on the topic.
8 In plenary, ask one group to report all their information and then let others add what has been left out.
9 Tell the class that you are about to read an article on the topic and ask them to be on the lookout for new information.

CHAPTER 6

# Poetic pretexts

## Using poems and songs

Because it is such a concentrated form of language, poetry spreads waves and ripples of thought. Good poems have a certain unity, depth and vividness which can awaken the creative powers of teacher and student alike. Patterns and repetitions, which occur naturally in poetry, are an indisputable aid to language acquisition.

This chapter offers ways of exploiting the colour of poetic language in reinforcing students' awareness of important language patterns.

**6.1**

**MATERIALS**
None

**LEVEL**
Advanced

**SKILLS**
Speaking; Reading; Writing; Interpretation

**TIME**
20–25 minutes

**SUGGESTED TEXTS**
Biography, autobiography or any text in which people are important

## THE BIO-POEM

Use this activity when you have a text which features interesting characters or when the personality of one character is of special importance. Your lesson will be more enjoyable and interesting if you can find an occasion or a place to display these poems if they are good, and they often are.

### Procedure

1 Ask the students if they have ever tried writing a poem. If any have, elicit the type and how they think poetry differs from other writing. (It's more concentrated, follows a pattern, has rhythm, etc.)
2 Tell the class that you want to try an experiment in writing poetry. You will be writing a 'bio-poem', that is, a poem describing someone's life or personality. Ask the students to imagine a person clearly in their minds. It may be someone they know, or a character from a book or film or even a historical figure. Pause for a short while to allow images to form.
3 Ask each student to write the name of their person. Wait for them to do this. Tell them that this name is the first line of their bio-poem. Tell them that the poem will have six lines and that they will be writing it line by line.
4 Line two of the poem is to consist of three adjectives describing the person, preferably adjectives starting with the same letter. You can help students find the right word by hinting or translating from the native language. This is also a good opportunity to introduce and use a synonym dictionary or a thesaurus.

Line three begins with the words *Who has loved...*
Line four begins with the words *Who wanted...*
Line five begins with the word *Always...* and has the word *never* in it.
Line six repeats the name of the person.
Each time you give instructions for the line, wait and allow students time to write. There will always be those who do not finish with the rest of the group. They should nevertheless continue with the class to the next line. Tell them that they will have more time later, to go back and complete unfinished lines.
Here is an example of a bio-poem:

Napoleon Bonaparte
Dashing, Daring, Defiant
Who has loved Josephine
Who wanted an empire
Always remembered... Never forgotten
Napoleon Bonaparte

5 In small groups, students read their poems to each other. Some of the poems are invariably about other class members. As a rule this is fun. Allow each group to choose one poem to be read out loud to the whole class.
6 Talk with the class about the difficulty of trying to define a person in writing and explain that in the text you are about to read personality is significant.

**VARIATION**

With a very imaginative class, you can ask students to suggest different patterns or line beginnings for the poems. They may wish to have the nationality of the character in one line, or their birthplace or parents, or perhaps they want line two and four to rhyme. Ask them to experiment.

**EXTENSION**

When you have finished reading the main text, ask the students to write bio-poems of the characters that appear in it.

## 6.2

**MATERIALS**
None

**LEVEL**
Advanced

**SKILLS**
Speaking; Writing; Asking questions

**TIME**
15–20 minutes

**SUGGESTED TEXTS**
Texts in which things are compared and contrasted

# THE CONTRAST POEM

One way in which we evaluate and measure the world around us is through comparison and contrast. Reading passages comparing geographical locations, places of work and social arrangements are found in the daily press, in magazines and frequently in EFL texts. *The contrast poem* eases students into the comparative/contrastive mode of such texts.

## Procedure

**1** Ask the students to remember a significant change in their lives. Facilitate this by recounting a change in your own life – perhaps your transition from the role of student to the role of teacher.

**2** Put the students in pairs and ask them to tell each other about this life change.

**3** Tell them that they will be writing poems that describe changed conditions in their lives. The poems will have only two lines.

The first line begins with:

*I used to...*

The second line begins with:

*But now I...*

They may add no more than five words to the first line and no more than ten to the second. For example:

I used to love eating ice cream
But now, I grow fat with each lick, my love has melted.

**4** Ask the students to sit in small groups and read their poems to each other. As each reader finishes, the other group members ask questions about their poem.

**5** Tell the students that they will read a text that also deals with comparisons and contrasts.

**VARIATION**

Instead of using, *I used to ... But now I ...*
You could use, *I have always wished ... But in real life ...*

# THE SINGLE IMAGE POEM

# 6.3

**MATERIALS**
None

**LEVEL**
Advanced

**SKILLS**
Speaking; Writing; Listening

**TIME**
15–20 minutes

**SUGGESTED TEXTS**
Any descriptive text

One of the great virtues of poetry is that it makes us see situations, predicaments and emotions through compact images. Thus, when Emily Dickinson tells us that 'Hope is the Thing with Feathers' (see page 37), an abstraction is linked to a clear, sharp picture. With a little practice, our students can create metaphorical images which will ease them into any descriptive text.

## Procedure

1 Write the following on the board:

Life is not a rose garden.
Each day is a blank page to write on.
Her emotions were a folded ironing board.
Their divorce was a broken egg.

2 Ask the students what two things have been compared in each case. Ask them why the comparisons are effective. If students do not consider them effective, they must explain why not. Point out or elicit the fact that one part of the comparison is abstract while the other is concrete.

3 Pair up the students and ask them to take one of the lines above and turn it into an image poem by adding another line. For example, 'Her emotions were a folded ironing board' could be turned into:

Her emotions were a folded ironing board
Everything was snapped shut.

Or 'Life is not a rose garden' could become:

Life is not a rose garden
It is more like a field of thistles.

4 In plenary, ask the pairs to read out their poems.

5 Ask the students to write their own image poems by comparing something abstract to something concrete. Tell them that the easiest way of doing this is to think of the concrete object first. For example, first think of a stove or an apple or a bicycle and then try to think of what abstract concept you can compare this to. For example, if you have thought of a bicycle, you know that it has two wheels that must move together. What can that make you think about? Perhaps a good marriage of long standing? There you have an image poem:

Joe and Sue – fifty years together
A bicycle struggling up the hillside, then gliding...gliding...

6 Ask students to read their poems to each other in small groups. Ask each group to vote for the best poem, which they can then read to the whole class.

7 Tell students that they will be reading a descriptive text and ask them to look for images similar to the ones in their poems.

## 6.4

**MATERIALS**
A few limericks to use as examples

**LEVEL**
Advanced

**SKILLS**
Speaking; Writing

**TIME**
15–20 minutes

**SUGGESTED TEXTS**
A unit of texts all dealing with the same theme

# THE LIMERICK

A limerick is a nonsense poem of five lines in which the first two lines rhyme and are followed by two more that rhyme differently and then by a fifth line that rhymes with the first two (a a b b a). Limericks were made popular by Edward Lear, a nineteenth-century British humourist and painter.

Writing limericks on a theme is fun and serves as a fine introduction to any unit based on one particular theme.

## Preparation

Find some limericks to use as examples, or use these:

There was an old man in a trunk
Who inquired of his wife, 'Am I drunk?'
She replied with remorse,
'Yes, darling, of course'
And he answered, 'That's just what I thunk'.

There was a young peasant named Gorse
Who fell madly in love with a horse
Said his wife, 'You rapscallion
That horse is a stallion
This constitutes grounds for divorce'.

## Procedure

1 Write the word *limerick* on the board and ask the students what they know about it. Such a form may exist in their native language. Be ready to explain the limerick form if you can't elicit the right details.
2 Read or hand out copies of limericks. Ask the students to read them and choose their favourites.
3 Tell them that they are going to read a group of texts dealing with a particular subject.
4 Elicit the ways in which a subject can be approached through sub-topics. Write the suggestions on the board. For example, if the subject is 'The Family', your list might include babies, divorce, money, teenagers, step-parents and grown-up children.
5 Divide the class into groups and ask them to write one or more limericks on one or more of the sub-topics they have just thought of. It is important to say *one or more* because in this way quick, creative groups might produce several limericks while the slower groups only write one. But every group will emerge with a product.
6 Listen to all the limericks and ask students to look out for examples of the theme they have written about as they go through the unit of texts.

# THE ACROSTIC

6.5

**MATERIALS**
None

**LEVEL**
Elementary +

**SKILLS**
Reading; Speaking; Writing

**TIME**
15–20 minutes

**SUGGESTED TEXTS**
Any text or group of texts based on a theme

An acrostic is a poem anyone can produce. I have used acrostics as introductions to texts with beginners' classes who had a fairly minimal vocabulary, but were willing to struggle a bit. The acrostic is a good headstart for a unit based on a certain theme, which is effectively used as the key word for the acrostic poem.

An acrostic poem is made by taking one word, such as *loneliness*, writing it vertically and using each of its letters to start a word, sentence or phrase related to the theme. For example:

L — Longing
O — Only for you
N — Never complete
E — Ever in agony
L — Longing
I — Inharmonious
N — Never complete
E — Ever in agony
S — Soul without soul
S — Self without self

## Preparation

Prepare one or two acrostics to show as examples. Write these on the board before you start the activity.

## Procedure

1 Tell the class that they will be reading some texts that are all based on the same theme A theme is like a basic melody, a recurring idea that is seen and felt in each text. The texts may be very different. One of them may be a story, one an essay and a third, perhaps, a poem, but the basic idea, the theme, will recur in all of them.
2 To check understanding, ask them which themes frequently occur in their daily newspaper. You might get answers such as 'violence', 'corruption' or 'politics'. In elementary monolingual classes students can answer in their native language. You can then elicit or provide translations.
3 Tell the students the theme of the texts you are about to read and write the word or words on the board.
4 Put the students in pairs and tell them that together they are to write an acrostic poem based on the theme word. Give them about three minutes to compose their acrostics. While they are working on them, walk about among the groups helping out with vocabulary and spelling.

5 When time is up, ask three pairs to get together, forming groups of six. In these groups, pairs read and, if necessary, explain their acrostics to each other. The listening pairs may ask questions. If there is a pair that has not succeeded in completing its acrostic, the rest of the group may help them do so.
6 Ask each group of six to pick its best acrostic. Ask a representative of each group to come to the front of the room.
7 Ask these representatives to sit, panel-style, in front of the class and read their acrostics.

ACKNOWLEDGEMENT
I learned this exercise from Laura, a creative teacher from Finland whose last name I have unfortunately forgotten. Laura participated in a workshop I was giving at Pilgrims at the University of Kent in Canterbury, England.

## 6.6

**MATERIALS**
Copies of a poem

**LEVEL**
Intermediate +

**SKILLS**
Reading; Explaining; Asking questions

**TIME**
5–10 minutes on day one
20–25 minutes on day two

**SUGGESTED TEXTS**
Poems

## ON YOUR OWN

This activity simply asks students to bring in their own favourite poems, read them and talk about them. Students, over the years, have brought in poems both in the native and the target language. Many have contributed nursery rhymes, lullabies, or pop songs. During this activity, I have heard the voices of students who, as a rule, remain totally passive.

### Preparation

Choose a favourite poem which is not too difficult. Prepare enough copies for the entire class. Practise reading it and be able to explain the poem and say why you like it.

### Procedure

DAY ONE

1 Put the words *poem* and *song* on the board. Ask the class how these are alike and how they are different. (In many languages the word for the two is the same.) Ask the class what happens to poems if they are turned into songs. (They usually become more well-known, but they may lose some of their original significance.) Listen to and accept all responses.
2 Ask the students if they have a favourite song or poem. If there are those who do, ask them what it is and why they like it. Ask if anyone had a favourite song or poem when they were young.

3 Tell the students about your favourite poem. Hand out copies of the poem and read it twice, dramatically, adding any interpretative commentary you wish. Tell the students why you like this poem.
4 Ask the students to bring in *their* own favourite song or poem for the next day. Tell them that, for homework, they should rehearse so they can read their poem well, be ready to explain it, and be able to say why they like it. The poem they bring in may be in either the native or the target language, but all the explanations and discussion must be in the target language.

DAY TWO
1 Divide the class into small groups.
2 Ask the students to read their poems to each other.
3 Everyone should explain their chosen poem and say why they like it. The listeners may ask questions after each reading.
4 Ask the students if there seem to be elements that all the poems and songs share. Elicit 'rhythm', 'rhyme', 'stress', 'concentration of ideas', 'repetition', etc.
5 Tell the students that over the next few lessons they will be reading poetry which involves much of what they have observed in today's readings.

## THE HAIKU

**6.7**

**MATERIALS**
Postcards showing nature scenes; pictures from travel magazines

**LEVEL**
Intermediate +

**SKILLS**
Writing; Speaking

**TIME**
15–20 minutes

**SUGGESTED TEXTS**
Any text dealing with or describing human emotions

The haiku is an eighteenth-century Japanese form of poetry. It is a three line poem which usually presents an object in nature and an emotion or a surprising observation that accompanies perception of that object.

Students can be inspired to produce their own haiku poems by looking at pictures. They can keep records of glimpses and flashes of things that have touched their emotional life, and with the help of the teacher, put such insights into words.

## Preparation

Learn how to explain the form of the haiku. Its structure is as follows:

First line – five syllables
Second line – seven to nine syllables
Third line – five syllables

For example:

A cluster of trees
And glint of the summer sea
The pale evening moon

Put this haiku, or any others you know, on the board before the lesson. Bring enough nature pictures for every student to have at least one.

## Procedure

**1** Write the word *haiku* on the board and ask if anyone has heard this word before and knows anything about it.
**2** If any students know the form ask them to explain. If no one knows the form explain it yourself. It is important to stress that the syllable rather than the word is the organisational form of the haiku. Make sure students understand what a syllable is. Practise counting syll-ables in such words as *different* (2 syllables) or *embarrasses* (4 syllables).
**3** Ask the students to read the haiku on the board and count the syllables in each line.
**4** Give each student a nature picture.
**5** Ask the students to study their picture for a few seconds and write down the first phrase or sentence that comes to mind.
**6** Ask them to expand the words into a haiku. As they do this, walk around helping with vocabulary, spelling and the counting of syll-ables. Remind them that this form of poetry fuses image with emotion.
**7** Ask the students in small groups to share their pictures and their haiku.
**8** Tell them that they are going to start reading a text dealing with emotions.

# PIECES IN PLACE

# 6.8

**MATERIALS**
Copies of the poem or song you are going to teach; A recording of the poem or song; A tape recorder

**LEVEL**
Advanced

**SKILLS**
Listening; Reading

**TIME**
15–20 minutes

**SUGGESTED TEXTS**
Any poem or song

This is a listening comprehension activity with a bit of surprise thrown in for spice. It can only be used once with each class, since the key element – of surprise – is lost the second time around. It's a fine introduction to the study of a song or a poem. I have used it to introduce several poems by Robert Frost, songs by the Beatles and John Lennon's 'Imagine'.

## Preparation

1 Duplicate enough copies of the poem or song to have one for each group. Cut the poem or song into strips of about half a stanza per strip. Put the strips into envelopes – one envelope for each group. Then duplicate another complete set. Do not cut these up but put them aside for later use.
2 Record yourself or a friend who performs well reading the poem. If you plan to teach a song, you will probably be able to find a professional recording.

## Procedure

1 Divide the class into groups of three to five and give each group an envelope of strips.
2 Tell them that each envelope contains pieces of a poem or a song that you plan to study with them.
3 Their task is to arrange the strips in the correct order. The group which finishes first wins.
4 As they get busy emptying out their envelopes and trying to decide what goes first, turn on, at a very low volume, the tape recording of the reading or song. Gradually turn up the volume.
5 Your students may not be aware of anything at first, but as you continue turning up the volume, someone will eventually notice hearing the words they have been trying to arrange and call other students' attention to it.
6 From then on, the activity turns into a careful listening comprehension. Play the tape several times until at least one group thinks that their strips are arranged just right.
7 Ask the group that finished first to read its version. Then replay the tape so that everyone can check. There will usually be a few mistakes.
8 Hand out the complete copies and begin intensive reading.

ACKNOWLEDGEMENT
I learned this familiar EFL activity from my friend and colleague Evie Azra, a gifted and dedicated teacher, textbook writer and teacher trainer.

## 6.9

**MATERIALS**
A recording of a song; Copies of the song, written as a cloze passage; A tape recorder

**LEVEL**
Elementary +

**SKILLS**
Vocabulary expansion; Intensive listening

**TIME**
10–15 minutes

**SUGGESTED TEXTS**
Any song

# FILLING SPACES

This is a musical version of the cloze. For less able students, one word spaces can be left to be filled in, while more able and creative classes can fill in entire lines. Songs by the Beatles are especially suitable for this activity. I usually ask students to bring in songs which they have on cassette at home but don't quite know or understand. The student who has brought in the song then helps me to compose the cloze passage.

## Preparation

1 Choose a suitable song and write the lyrics as a cloze passage, leaving blank spaces for words, phrases or sentences.
2 Duplicate enough copies so that you have one for each student.

## Procedure

1 Give out the cloze passage song sheet.
2 Read it out loud, pausing briefly at the blank spaces.
3 Ask one or two students to do the same.
4 Ask the students to write any word, phrase or sentence (depending on what you have left out) that they consider appropriate in the blanks.
5 Ask the students to sit in small groups and compare what they have put into the blanks. Ask each group to produce one complete song by choosing the best of all their individual answers and combining them.
6 Unless your class is very large, ask each group to read out its composition. In very large classes, only listen to those groups who volunteer their efforts.
7 Play the song. Ask students to listen for, and write, the words, phrases or sentences above their own in the blank spaces. You will probably have to listen two or three times before everyone has been able to note down the required vocabulary.
8 Ask the students to compare their versions with the correct one.

# POETIC GATEWAY

## 6.10

**MATERIALS**
Copies of a poem

**LEVEL**
Advanced

**SKILLS**
Reading;
Interpreting;
Speaking

**TIME**
20–25 minutes

**SUGGESTED TEXTS**
Any longer texts, thematically arranged

*Poetic gateway* involves use of a serious and thoughtful poem as an entrance to a longer text, a unit of texts, or a longer extensive reading on one theme. Throughout the later readings, I continue to refer back to the original poem. This gives the entire unit a sense of structure and purpose.

## Preparation

Choose a thoughtful, serious poem which deals with the theme later to be considered in the unit. Practise reading it well.

## Procedure

1 Read the poem out loud twice.
2 Ask students to describe the central character or plot of the poem. What does the poet actually make us see, feel, hear or smell? In the poem 'The Road not Taken' by Robert Frost (below), we see a man walking in an autumnal wood. He sees a path diverging in two directions and he ponders which way to go. I would want my students to see this picture *very clearly*. I would want them to visualise the leafiness and subdued sunshine of the woods. I would want them to see the man as he walks, head bent down in thought. I would want them to hear birds chirping in the tree tops above the man.

The Road not Taken

Two roads diverged in a yellow wood
And sorry I could not travel both
And be one traveller, long I stood
And looked down one as far as I could
To where it bent in the undergrowth;
Then took the other as just as fair,
And having perhaps the better claim,
Because it was grassy and wanted wear;
Though as for that the passing there
Had worn them really about the same.

And both that morning equally lay
In leaves no step had trodden black.
Oh, I kept the first for another day!
Yet knowing how way leads on to way
I doubted if I should ever come back.
I shall be telling this with a sigh
Somewhere ages and ages hence:
Two roads diverged in the wood, and I –
I took the one less travelled by,
And that has made all the difference.

From *The Poetry of Robert Frost*, Holt Rinehart and Winston, 1979, p. 105

3 Hand out copies of the poem. Ask the students to read it, underlining what they consider to be the most important lines. As they read, answer any questions about vocabulary.
4 Ask the students to sit in small groups and tell each other which lines they have chosen and why.
5 Ask various students which lines they chose and write these on the board. There will be a lot of repetition. From 'The Road not Taken', students usually choose:
'Oh, I kept the first for another day!' (line 13)
'I doubted if I should ever come back' (line 15)
'I took the one less travelled by' (line 19)
'And that has made all the difference' (line 20)
6 Ask the students to say how the meaning or message of the whole poem can be seen in the lines written on the board. Listen to all their ideas. In 'The Road not Taken' we reach the conclusion that the poet is explaining why decisions are difficult.
7 Elicit more comments on the central message.
8 After some minutes of this discussion, tell the class that they will be reading further texts which relate to this central question.

**NOTE**

Here are some suggestions for poems and the subject matter they could relate to.
'Out Out' by Robert Frost, for a unit on accidents or child labour.
'The Road not Taken' by Robert Frost, for a unit on decisions.
'Ozymandias' by Percy Bysshe Shelley, for a unit connected with vanity and pride.
'Richard Corey' by Edwin Arlington Robinson, for a unit dealing with misunderstanding, lack of communication or jealousy.
'Phizzog' by Carl Sandburg, for a unit dealing with personal identity.
'Ballade of Lost Objects' by Phyllis McGinley, for a unit on growing up.

# CHAPTER 7

# *Naming is taming*

## *Using names and titles*

Names and titles are important both to readers and writers. A good title does more than just attract our attention. It conveys a mysterious sense of meaning and reverberates with clues about what will happen in the text. Some titles are deliberately made to mislead us, some are there to keep us guessing throughout the whole text. Names of characters, just like names of people, are part and parcel of their identity. This chapter shows ways of using naming in language learning.

## IT SITS WHERE IT FITS

**7.1**

**MATERIALS**
Several copies of the same newspaper

**LEVEL**
Intermediate +

**SKILLS**
Predicting; Brainstorming; Scanning; Reading

**TIME**
15–20 minutes

**SUGGESTED TEXTS**
Newspapers and magazines

This is a matching activity with the added component of guessing. For it to work successfully, you must remember that there are no wrong answers during the discussion of which headline matches which paragraph, as long as students give a good reason for naming a paragraph. Remember that your goal is lots of interesting talk and speculation, and not 'correct' answers.

### Preparation

Take one copy of the newspaper which you are about to read with the class and cut out as many headlines as there will be small groups in the class. These headlines should be fairly cryptic. In other words, it should not be obvious from the headline what the article is about. For example, the headline 'Storm over South America!' could refer to a political or economic storm.

Cut out the opening paragraphs of the articles from which you have taken the headlines. Arrange these on one page and photocopy enough of these pages to have one for each group.

### Procedure

1 Divide the class into groups and give each group one headline. Ask them to brainstorm as many possible subjects of the article as they can in three to five minutes.
2 Ask each group to read out their headline and their list of possible subjects. As each group finishes, ask the remainder of the class to contribute other options. Write all the headlines on the board.

3 Hand each group a copy of the sheet with the first paragraphs. Their task is to match paragraph with headline. Tell them that there are no 'right' answers but that they must justify their choice.
4 In plenary, the groups explain their matching. Accept all variations and possibilities, as long as they are justified.
5 Hand out the newspapers and allow students to locate the headlines and texts which they have just been talking about. Ask them if anything surprises them, and discuss the fact that headlines often are misleading.

**VARIATION**

At Step 1, instead of giving each group a different headline, give the same headline to two different groups. It is always interesting to see how differently two groups interpret the same bit of text.

## 7.2 SCRAMBLED GUESSING

**MATERIALS**
Index cards

**LEVEL**
Advanced

**SKILLS**
Predicting; Guessing; Speaking

**TIME**
10–15 minutes

**SUGGESTED TEXTS**
Short stories or articles with complex titles

This is particularly suitable if your text is a short story with a long and mysterious name – one with no fewer than four words in the title. I used this activity for two short stories I taught. One written by Flannery O'Connor called, 'Everything that Rises must Converge', and the other by Tillie Olsen called 'I Stand Here Ironing'. I scrambled the title of the first story to: 'Converge must that rises everything', and the second to 'Ironing stand here I'.

### Preparation

Scramble the words in the title of the story or article. Write the scrambled title on some index cards. Provide one card for each small group.

### Procedure

1 Divide your class into small groups.
2 Give each group the same scrambled title. Tell them that they are going to read a story/article that has a title in which all the words that you have given them on the card appear but that the words are not in the correct order. Their task is to rearrange the words in a plausible order.
3 Elicit suggestions. Ask if any group has changed its mind about the title now that they have heard from other groups. If any group has changed its mind, it may adopt the title of another group.
4 Each group now brainstorms as many ideas as possible about the content of the story. This may be what they think will happen in one story, or suggestions about possible stories that could grow out of such a title.

For example, for the title 'Everything that Rises must Converge':

i This could be a story about a poor boy who wants to marry a rich girl. Her family is against it. As they mature, the boy becomes a millionaire while the girl's family loses all its money. The two eventually get it together and there is a happy romance.

ii This could be a story about meeting after death, about a car accident or a renunion of snobs, or else it could be about rising prices or social climbing.

5 In plenary, listen to all the possibilities. Tell students not to forget their guesses as they progress through the story.

## CALL IT BY NAME

7.3

**MATERIALS**
One copy of a daily newspaper in the target language

**LEVEL**
Intermediate +

**SKILLS**
Discussion; Headline writing

**TIME**
10–15 minutes

**SUGGESTED TEXTS**
Newspaper articles

This activity involves analysis of headlines. Headlines are written according to rules different from those of 'normal' language. They are frequently incomplete sentences. They tend to use nouns instead of verbs and vice versa. Their primary function is to attract attention which they will do, even if this involves a trick or two that might mislead the reader. Headlines must give a great deal of information in a limited space and must scream without repelling.

### Procedure

1. Tell the class that you have just bought today's newspaper, but haven't yet had time to look at it. Ask them if they can help you guess what the stories in it might be about. Write their suggestions on the board.
2. Divide the class into groups and ask each group to choose one of the topics that have been written on the board and create a headline for it. Allow two minutes for this activity, and then ask the groups to read out their headlines.
3. Show the class the front page of the newspaper and compare the real headlines with those written by the students. Ask, 'How is the language of headlines different from normal language?' Write the responses on the board.
4. Tell the class that they will be reading an article about a particular subject. Briefly summarise the contents of the text.
5. Ask the students to form new small groups and make headlines for the article you will be reading. Walk around the class helping out with vocabulary. When one group has five headlines, stop the activity.
6. In plenary, ask each group to read out its headlines. Praise those with appropriate headline language and originality.

## 7.4

**MATERIALS**
Copies of a list of possible titles for the story to be read

**LEVEL**
Intermediate +

**SKILLS**
Discussion;
Explaining;
Predicting

**TIME**
15–20 minutes

**SUGGESTED TEXTS**
Any fictional story

# BEST CHOICE

This activity involves a great deal of discussion and explanation about making a choice of the correct title for a story.

## Preparation

**1** Make up six to eight possible titles for the story you are going to read. Some should be ridiculous, some appropriate and some bland. Among them include the real title. For example, if I was planning to teach the story *Cinderella*, I might write the following:

Only a Glass Slipper
From the Kitchen to the Ball Room
Trust A Fairy Godmother
Goodness Rewarded
It Pays to Have Small Feet
Cinderella
Cinder-Princess

**2** Write the titles on a sheet of paper and make enough copies to give one to each group.

## Procedure

**1** Tell the class you are going to read a story. Briefly summarise the contents of the first half of the story. For example, for *Cinderella* you might say:

The story is about a widower with a young daughter who married a woman who had two daughters from her previous marriage. This woman and her daugters soon began to abuse the man's only child, who was not given proper clothing or any opportunity to socialise. She didn't even have a bed of her own, but slept in the cinders in the fireplace since that was the only warm spot in the house. This poor child grew very depressed and she felt especially miserable one evening when her whole family went off to a ball at the Royal Palace and she was left in the house, alone and sad . . .

**2** Divide the class into small groups.
**3** Give each group a title paper. They have two tasks:
**i** Write the end of the story.
**ii** Choose, from the list, the most appropriate title for *their* story. Everyone in the group must agree.
**4** In plenary, ask the groups to read out their titles and story endings.
**5** When students start reading the real story, there is always some kind of a reaction when the actual title is revealed. Some teachers prefer to present the story without a title and not reveal it until the class has finished reading the whole story.

## LINKS IN A CHAIN

## 7.5

**MATERIALS**
Copies of an article

**LEVEL**
Intermediate +

**SKILLS**
Reading; Summarising; Taking notes; Predicting

**TIME**
15–20 minutes

**SUGGESTED TEXTS**
Any article or essay

This works best in more able classes and suits the kind of student who can make sense of an isolated fragment of a larger text. The activity also demands some summarising skills. Personally, I like this activity best with newspaper articles or essays, since the individual paragraphs tend to function as semi-independent units, but some teachers also report having used the activity successfully with short stories.

### Preparation

Cut the article up into four sections. If you have a very large class, photocopy the article and have eight sections.

### Procedure

1 Divide the class into four groups of four to seven students.
2 Give a different section of the article to one student in each group. Tell the student to read it out loud to the rest of their group twice. The other students in the groups take notes on the main ideas and together summarise the contents of their bit of text.
3 Ask the groups to give their bit of text a title. Stress that a good title must be short, refer to the contents and attract attention.
4 Ask each group to read out its title. Write them all on the board.
5 Ask the students to stay in the same groups and, in their groups, arrange the titles on the board into what they think is the same order as the paragraphs in the article. They write this on a sheet of paper.
6 From the hints given by their titles and their sequence on the board, ask the students to predict the contents of the whole article.
7 Tell them to keep their various points of disagreement in mind as they read the complete text.

## 7.6

**MATERIALS**
None

**LEVEL**
Advanced

**SKILLS**
Discussion;
Predicting

**TIME**
10–15 minutes

**SUGGESTED TEXTS**
Any fiction text with prominent characters

# WHO IS WHO?

Where did we get our names? Some of us were named after a beloved relative, some because of a momentary fancy of our parents, some because of an historical event. Many of us have hated the names given to us – some have even changed them. No matter how we feel about our name, it has inescapably become a part of our identity. Writers, as a rule, do not name their characters without a great deal of thought. The name of a character in a work of fiction reverberates with thematic and symbolic significance. *Who is who?* asks students to create mental images for characters they have not yet met, simply from associations with their names.

## Preparation

Read through the text making a list of the names of the important characters. Write these names on the board before the lesson starts.

## Procedure

1 Tell the class that they will be reading a story and that its cast of characters appears on the board.
2 Divide the class into small groups.
3 Tell them that each group must choose one name from the board. Their task then is to decide the following:
   - How old is this person?
   - What does this person look like?
   - What occupation does this person have?
   - How does this person relate to other people?
4 In plenary, ask each group to introduce its character. This part becomes interesting if two groups have chosen the same name and created a completely different image for that character.
5 Tell the students to look for their character in the text as they start reading.

## UPSIDE DOWN WHO IS WHO?

## 7.7

**MATERIALS**
Copies of a description of each major character that appears in the text

**LEVEL**
Elementary +

**SKILLS**
Explaining; Predicting

**TIME**
10–15 minutes

**SUGGESTED TEXTS**
Short stories or novels

Names change just like fashions in clothing. The name Bertha, for example, which today for unknown reasons, conjures up girth, was perceived as a glamorous name in the nineteenth-century novel. In all cultures and languages names of flowers or animals abound in the nursery only to be replaced a generation later by names from a culture's holy writings or literature or popular movies. I have found this activity particularly interesting in multilingual, multicultural classes, where students were willing to share their culture's special idiosyncrasies regarding names.

### Preparation

1 Prepare a handout which gives a description of each major character in the text. Do not give names or labels to any of the descriptions. For example, if I were writing a description of Cinderella's father, I might write:

   A middle-class, middle-aged man who has lost his first wife and remarried. He seems to be an extremely weak person as he does nothing to help his own daughter when she is abused by his new wife and that wife's daughters.

2 Before the lesson starts, write the following questions on the board:

   1 Do you like your own name?
   2 Why were you given the name you have?
   3 Does your name have a meaning?
   4 Is your name popular in your culture?
   5 Which are your favourite English names?

### Procedure

1 Ask the students to read the questions on the board.
2 Divide the class into small groups and ask the students to tell each other the answers to the questions.
3 Elicit group reports of favourite English names. Write these names on the board.
4 Give each group one of the lists of descriptions. Tell them that these are descriptions of characters they will meet in the story they are about to read. Ask them to name the people described. They may use names from the board or other names, but these should all be English names. Each group should try to reach a consensus.
5 In plenary, elicit reports on how they named the characters. With each naming try to get an explanation. There will be a great deal of disagreement among groups. Encourage them to explain why they disagree.
6 Use a bridge sentence such as: 'You have chosen interesting names for these people. Now let's see which names the writer has chosen. Let's see if you recognise the characters from my descriptions'.

## 7.8

**MATERIALS**
None

**LEVEL**
Advanced

**SKILLS**
Speaking;
Predicting

**TIME**
10–15 minutes

**SUGGESTED TEXTS**
Short stories and articles

# DIVIDE AND CONQUER

This works well if you are teaching either a short story or an article that has a title which consists of two distinct components. I have used this introduction to an article from the New York Times entitled 'Apples and South Africa', as well as to a short story by Bernard Malamud called, 'A Summer's Reading'. With the article my two components were 'Apples' and 'South Africa'. For the Malamud story I used 'Summer' and 'Reading' as components.

## Preparation

Divide the title of the story/article you are going to read into two components.

## Procedure

1 Divide the class into two groups of eight to twelve students. If your class is very large, make four groups. Ask each group to appoint a secretary.
2 Give each group one word which constitutes one component of the title. If you have four groups, two groups should be given the same component and the other two groups the second component.
3 The task of the groups is to brainstorm for any ideas associated with the word given to them. The secretary takes notes of all the ideas.
4 In plenary, listen to ideas contributed by all the groups.
5 Ask the class if they can see any connection between the two components.
6 Allow students to think and don't worry if it takes a while for answers to come. They will come eventually – some that you, yourself, would never have dreamed of. Let the ideas flow. If there is a silence for a while, wait, more ideas are on the way.
7 Tell the class that the two components are parts of the title of the story/article you are going to read. Ask them to watch for how the writer has connected the two ideas.

ACKNOWLEDGEMENT
This activity was worked out by my co-author, Evelyn Azra and me as we worked on our book *It Stands to Reason* (Eric Cohen Books, 1988).

## WHICH IS WHICH?

This is a guessing and prediction activity involving jumbled-up word strings made up of the title of the text and parts of the first and last sentences.

**7.9**

**MATERIALS**
None

**LEVEL**
Intermediate +

**SKILLS**
Predicting; Discussion

**TIME**
10–15 minutes

**SUGGESTED TEXTS**
Any text

### Preparation

On the board write the title of the text you are going to read, the first five words, and the last three words of the text. All of this should be mixed together in one piece of writing. For example, for 'Eveline' (a story by James Joyce), the first five words are, 'She sat at the window'. The last three words are, 'Farewell or recognition'. I might write, 'Farewell or recognition Eveline she sat at the window'. Or this, 'Eveline farewell she sat at the window recognition'. Or any other combination.

### Procedure

1 Tell the class that what you have written on the board may look like nonsense but that it is actually a combination of three things – the title of a story they are going to read, the first five words of that story and the three last words as well.
2 Divide the class into small groups. They have two tasks. Firstly to break the words on the board down into their three components (title, first five words, last three words). Then to predict the content of the story.
3 In plenary, listen to all the groups' reports. Then give them the real title, the first five words and the last three words. Ask them whether they have changed their minds about the content of the story.

## 7.10

**MATERIALS**
None

**LEVEL**
Intermediate +

**SKILLS**
Predicting;
Listening;
Summarising

**TIME**
15–20 minutes

**SUGGESTED TEXTS**
Any text with a mysterious title

# CRYPTIC TITLE

A mysterious title to a story, article, essay or poem is ideal for sparking interest. However, the activity frequently falls flat when teachers just say, 'That's a strange name for a story, what do you think it could be about?' The lack of enthusiasm on the part of students comes from the weak structure in such completely open-ended guessing. I have found that simply adding an extra element to the guessing can make all the difference.

## Preparation

1 Choose some details from the text to tell the class.
2 Write the title of the text on the board.

## Procedure

1 Tell the class that what you have written on the board is the title of a text they are going to read and elicit /explain any difficult vocabulary in the title. Then tell them about the text. For example, I have used this introduction to a story by Flannery O'Connor which goes by the mysterious title of 'Everything that Rises must Converge'. I tell the class that this is a story about a difficult relationship between a mother and her grown-up son. The story takes place in the fifties in the south of the United States of America. Racial prejudice is also part of the story.
2 Divide the class into small groups (three to five students per group). Ask them to review the information you have told them from the story and write a brief summary of it.
3 In plenary, ask one group to write their summary on the board. Ask other groups to think of anything forgotten by this group and add this to the information on the board.
4 Ask the students to regroup into other small groups. The task of these groups is to find connections between the title and the additional information they have been given.
5 Ask them to keep these ideas in mind as they read the text. At the end of the reading, analyse the title again. In many texts the title remains abstruse even after the reading. This is, of course, more food for discussion.

CHAPTER 8

# Talk to the text

## *Using interactive techniques*

How often has a book cheered you up or made you angry or perhaps even depressed you? Are you one of those people who insists on writing comments in the margins of the texts you read? The text-centred foreign language class should provide a few opportunities to exercise such a universal need to talk back to the text.

## GUT REACTIONS

8.1

**MATERIALS**
Copies of one paragraph from the text

**LEVEL**
Intermediate +

**SKILLS**
Reading; Listening; Paragraph writing; Predicting; Skimming

**TIME**
20–30 minutes

**SUGGESTED TEXTS**
Stories, novels, articles

*Gut reactions* seems like a long and complex activity. Really it's very simple to do and requires almost no preparation on the part of the teacher. The activity works well as an introduction to a longer text or a text which is to be read extensively. The activity fosters class intimacy since it involves a great deal of sharing and introspection.

### Preparation

From a longer text which you plan to read with the class pick one paragraph and make a class set of copies.

### Procedure

1 Give each student a copy of the paragraph. Ask them to read it and find in it one sentence which they agree with completely, or disagree with or find amusing, or upsetting or ridiculous or a sentence that in *any* way speaks to them on an emotional level. Ask everyone to underline their sentence.
2 In groups of four, students read the sentence they have chosen to each other and explain why they have chosen it. Tell them to listen carefully because you will later be asking them to report on each other's choices.
3 Ask various students to read out loud one sentence a member of their group chose, and explain why. The reports from groups should not come from the person who chose the sentence, but rather from someone who listened. For example, 'Margaret chose sentence ______. She said that it made her angry because...'
Each time such a sentence is read ask 'Margaret' to verify whether or not she agrees with what was reported. Write all the reported sentences on the board.

It is interesting to note that in some groups all four students will have chosen the same sentence, with different reactions to it, while in other groups everyone will have chosen something different.

**4** Collect the paragraphs. Ask students to look at the sentences on the board and to try to recreate the paragraph using these sentences. Listen to several of the recreated paragraphs. Ask the class if anything has been missed, changed, or added.

**5** Ask the class to predict what the complete text will be about.

**6** Hand out the full text and ask the class to skim it until they find the particular paragraph which they have been working on.

**VARIATION**

If you have a very intellectual class, ask students to translate the passage into their native language (between Steps 5 and 6). Ask students to read out and comment on the translated versions. Since every translation is also an interpretation, I have always found such discussions useful and interesting.

## 8.2 WHY, WHERE AND HOW?

**MATERIALS**
None

**LEVEL**
Intermediate +

**SKILLS**
Asking questions; Dictation; Predicting

**TIME**
15–20 minutes

**SUGGESTED TEXTS**
Short fiction

Every reader approaches a text full of questions. Am I going to enjoy this book? Will I understand it? Will it be a waste of my time? Will I learn something new from it? This activity attempts to capitalise on this curiosity.

### Procedure

**1** Dictate the first paragraph of a story you are going to read with the class, or ask a student who is a good reader to dictate it.

**2** Divide your class into small groups of five or six. Ask each group to appoint a secretary. The task of each group is to make up as many questions as possible which relate to this paragraph and to what they imagine might be the further development of the story. At least one of the questions must begin with *Where*, one with *Why* and one with *How*. For example, the first paragraph of the story 'Eveline' by James Joyce, which I frequently teach is:

> She sat by the window watching the evening invade the avenue. Her head was leaned against the window curtains, and in her nostrils was the odour of dusty cretonne. She was tired.

From 'Eveline', a short story in *The Dubliners*, James Joyce, Jonathan Cape, 1967, p. 37.

Questions made up by students on such a paragraph include:

Why is she so tired?
How old is she?
Where does this story take place?
Why is she sitting by the window?
Is she waiting for someone?
Where does she work?
What does she look like?
Why does she seem so sad?
Is she afraid of anything?
Is she alone?
Is she rich or poor?

As students make out questions, circulate to help out with vocabulary and question formation.

**3** Collect the questions from each group and pass them on to another group.

**4** Each group attempts to answer the questions passed on to them, thereby predicting the contents of the story.

**5** In plenary, listen to questions and answers from several groups. Invite other groups to contribute interesting questions and answers. For examples a group member might say, 'Our group has got a question we can't answer.' The teacher can reply, 'Well, let's hear it. Maybe someone else can answer it ...'

**6** Tell the students to keep their questions and answers in mind as they read through the text.

## 8.3

**MATERIALS**
Hat or bag in which to collect question strips; Index cards

**LEVEL**
Intermediate +

**SKILLS**
Asking questions; Predicting; Writing; Dictation

**TIME**
10–15 minutes

**SUGGESTED TEXTS**
Short stories or novels

# WHY DO THEY DO IT?

In fiction, as in life, people fall in love, buy and sell things, marry the wrong person, drop out of school at a bad time and choose the wrong career. This activity invites students to interact with the text by searching for what motivates certain characters to act or behave as they do.

## Preparation

Write a very short description, no more than a few lines, about the qualities and actions of the characters in the story.

For example, if my story were *Cinderella*, my list of characters might look like this:

1 **The father.** He marries a second wife. He does nothing to help his daughter. He seems very passive.
2 **Stepmother.** She is a social climber. She marries for the second time. She is very cruel to her stepdaughter. She does not seem very considerate of her husband.
3 **Stepsisters.** They seem very much alike. They are vain. They are social climbers who will do almost anything, even mutilate themselves physically, to get ahead in society.
4 **Cinderella.** She is good and obedient. She seems very passive. She is modest and beautiful. Her goodness is rewarded.

Write each description on a separate index card or piece of paper.

## Procedure

1 Hand the description cards to students who are good readers. Ask each of them to pick a partner, who will be their writer.
2 The pairs go to the board, where each reader dictates to their writer, who writes on the board while the rest of the class copies all the descriptions. Explain any problem words.
3 Divide the class into small groups and ask each group to look over the list of character descriptions they have copied. Ask them to choose one character from the list and make up as many questions as possible about this character. All the questions must begin with the word *Why*. Each question should be written on a separate slip of paper. Possible questions on the above characters might be:

   - Why doesn't Cinderella complain to her father?
   - Why does the stepmother marry for the second time?
   - Why don't the stepsisters befriend Cinderella?

   While they do this walk around helping with vocabulary and question formation.
4 Collect all the slips of paper in a bag or hat.
5 Walk among the groups, asking each group to pick one slip from the bag. If they pull out one of their own slips, they should put it back and

try for another. Their task is to answer the questions on it in as many ways as possible. For example, if they got a question which asked 'Why was Cinderella's father so passive?' they might answer:

- He had a bossy mother.
- He was a lazy person.
- He wasn't healthy.
- He was optimistic and believed that everything would work out.
- His own father had been a drunkard who mistreated his mother. So he wanted to be good to his own wife.

6 Ask each group to read out their questions and answers. Tell them to be on the lookout for what motivates people as they read the story.

## ASK AWAY

**8.4**

**MATERIALS**
None

**LEVEL**
Intermediate +

**SKILLS**
Asking questions; Scanning; Predicting

**TIME**
15–20 minutes

**SUGGESTED TEXTS**
Any text

This activity gets students to interact with the text while reviewing question-asking. It is an activity that gets going easily and picks up momentum quickly. It should proceed briskly and not be allowed to drag.

### Procedure

1 Ask the students to glance through the text they are about to read. If the text is a section of their textbook, just direct them to the right pages. Ask them to find *any* complete sentence in the text and copy it out, then close their books.

2 Divide the class into small groups of five to seven. Each group appoints a secretary. Each group member reads their sentence and as soon as they have read it, the others in the group ask as many questions as possible based on the sentence. The questions can be as silly or as serious as anyone wants to make them. The only requirement is that they are somehow connected to the original sentence. For example, if one student's sentence is, 'Grandfather visited us last week,' some possible questions could be:

When did Grandfather visit you?
Why did Grandfather visit you?
How long will he stay?
Did Grandmother come too?
Why didn't he come sooner?
Why last week?
Why doesn't he live with you?
Did he bring presents?

3 As soon as the group has run out of questions, the secretary writes down the name of the student who presented the sentence and the number of questions asked about it.
4 Ask for the highest number of questions that was elicited in each group and write the sentences which brought out the most questions on the board.
5 Bring the whole class back together and ask the students to guess at the content of the text from the sentences on the board, as well as from other sentences they heard in their groups.
6 Tell the students to look out for the sentences they have been working on while they read the text.

## 8.5 NEIGHBOURS

**MATERIALS**
Copies of character descriptions from the text

**LEVEL**
Advanced

**SKILLS**
Speaking

**TIME**
15–20 minutes

**SUGGESTED TEXTS**
Short stories or novels

While gossip is considered evil by some, it is looked on by others as innocent interest in other people. Look at it any way you wish, the fact is that it exists and its clear and simple discourse makes it a good model for the EFL classroom.

### Preparation

Write brief descriptions of several characters that appear in the text you are going to be reading with your class. Write all the descriptions on one sheet of paper and photocopy it so that you have one copy for each pair of students.

### Procedure

1 Ask the students to sit in pairs and give each pair the list of character descriptions. Each pair should study the list and pick one character they think neighbours might want to gossip about.
2 Once each pair has picked its character, their task is to make a list of good and bad things that can be said about that person. While they do this, circulate among the pairs helping out with vocabulary and ideas. For example, if a pair has chosen Cinderella's father as their character they could write, 'He is gentle, he is good to his wife and stepdaughters, he is generous . . .' On his negative side, they might write, 'He is passive, he allows his own daughter to be abused, he rushed into marriage too early before he really knew his second wife well . . .'
3 Ask several pairs to read their lists of character qualities out loud.
4 Ask each pair to role play two neighbours gossiping about the character they have chosen. One neighbour says nasty things about the character, the other contradicts this by giving the positive qualities of the character. Circulate, listening to their role plays.

5 If you see one pair doing a particularly good job, you may wish to ask them to do a repeat performance in front of the whole class.
6 Tell the class that they will meet their characters in the text they are about to read.

## OPPOSITE DICTATION

## 8.6

**MATERIALS**
One copy of a rewritten 'opposite paragraph' for each group

**LEVEL**
Intermediate +

**SKILLS**
Listening; Dictation; Skimming

**TIME**
15–20 minutes

**SUGGESTED TEXTS**
Any text

This is an enjoyable activity simply because everyone has a different idea of what 'opposite' means. For example, if I asked you the opposite of the word *girl*, you might automatically say *boy*. Under other circumstances you might think the opposite of *girl* is *woman* or *sophisticated lady*, or if you think of the word *girl* in terms of *servant* the opposite would be *mistress*. This, I have discovered over years of teaching, can be done with almost any word. Is the opposite of *waiter waitress* or is it *customer, guest, client, restaurant owner or head waiter*? It all depends on circumstances, doesn't it?

### Preparation

Find a short easy paragraph in the text you plan to teach and rewrite it, turning as many words as possible into what you, at the time of reading, perceive as their opposites. For example:

Original paragraph

There once was a very rich old man whose name I don't want to mention here because it must still be kept a secret, who one day decided that he would leave all his money to his niece. I don't know what made him decide such a thing, because Sara, his niece, had always been a spoiled ungrateful brat who never spent five minutes with her uncle.

Opposite paragraph

There never was a poor young woman, whose name I want to shout out because everyone should know it, who one night came on the idea of not leaving any of her money to her nephew. I do know what made her dream of such a thing because Sam, her nephew, had never been an unspoiled well-behaved child who always spent hours of time with his aunt.



Make one copy of the rewritten 'opposite paragraph' for each group in the class.

## Procedure

**1** Divide the class into small groups.
**2** Give the paragraph to a good reader in each group.
**3** Ask the reader to dictate the paragraph slowly to the group, pausing whenever asked.
**4** The students writing the paragraph should listen to what is said, but not write what they hear. They should instead write the *opposite*. Stress to them that they need not worry about whether or not this makes sense.
**5** When the dictation is finished, each person in each group should read their opposite paragraph to their group. This is great fun as the opposites are often quite different.
**6** Tell them that the original paragraph dictated to them was the opposite of a paragraph in the text they are going to read. Ask them to skim the text trying to find the paragraph you had chosen.

**VARIATION**
For less capable classes, use the original paragraph in the group dictation rather than turning it into an opposite paragraph. This, of course, saves you some work.

ACKNOWLEDGEMENT
This activity is a variation of one I learned from Tessa Woodward in a course I took from her in the summer of 1986 at Pilgrims at the University of Kent, Canterbury, England.

## 8.7 A WORD OF ADVICE

**MATERIALS**
Copies of list of hopes and ambitions

**LEVEL**
Intermediate +

**SKILLS**
Speaking; Giving advice; Explaining

**TIME**
10–15 minutes

**SUGGESTED TEXTS**
Long or short fiction

This activity asks students to interact with characters from fiction. Once they start reading the text, they will identify with the writer's point of view and lose their neutrality, but *before* they encounter the text, you can tell them about the dreams, ambitions and hopes of the characters they are going to meet and ask the students to offer them advice on how these ambitions can best be fulfilled.

## Preparation

Go through the text making notes of the characters' hopes, ambitions and expectations. On your list, write the name of the character, a brief description and their hopes, dreams, or ambitions written out in the form of an 'I want ...' sentence. Do not put more than four characters on your list. For example, using *Cinderella* as a text:

Cinderella, young woman, 'I want to have nice clothes, friends and love.'
Cinderella's father, a middle-aged man who has just remarried, 'I want peace and quiet in the house. I want everyone to get along.'

Cinderella's Stepmother, middle-aged woman with two daughters from former marriage, 'I want to get ahead in the world. I want my daughters to marry well.'

## Procedure

1 Give each student a copy of the list and ask them to read it. Tell them that they will meet these characters in the story they are going to read. Tell them to consider the ambitions of these characters and make notes on the kind of advice one could give people with such ambitions. Students may ask you various things like, 'Do they have money?' 'Where do they live?' Tell them that these questions are, for the moment, open. They may assume anything they want to about these people.
   Ask each student to make notes on the advice they would give. It might be helpful to write a list of useful structures on the board, for example:
   *Perhaps she should ...*
   *He could ...*
   *He may try to ...*
   *If he tries to ...*
   *She ought to ...*
   *He really must ...*
2 Ask the students to sit in small groups and share the advice they have given to the characters.
3 In plenary, listen to the advice from several groups and tell them to look out for these ambitions as they read the text.

# EXPECTATIONS

## 8.8

**MATERIALS**
None

**LEVEL**
Elementary +

**SKILLS**
Asking questions

**TIME**
5–10 minutes

**SUGGESTED TEXTS**
Any text

*Expectations* is a quick activity for readers who want to know what to expect from the text they are about to read. It is good for revising question-asking.

## Preparation

Write the following words, and/or any other words you think may be useful, on the board:

| | |
|---|---|
| amuse | learn |
| entertain | find out |
| pleasure | excite |
| suspense | interesting |
| information | boring |
| knowledge | difficult |

In very able classes, you need not put any words on the board.

## Procedure

1 Divide the class into small groups.
2 Ask each group to appoint a secretary.
3 Tell the students that they are about to start reading a new text and since they know nothing about it, you would like them to make up some questions about it. Tell them that the words on the board are there to help them get ideas about the kind of questions they might ask, but that they need not necessarily use these words. Everyone in the group should contribute questions and the secretary should write them down. They might come up with questions such as:

   Will the text have much new interesting information?
   Will there be a test after we finish reading the text?
   Is the text amusing?
   Will I be able to talk to my family about the information in this text?
   Will there be a lot of homework on this text?
   Is it a boring text?
   Is it a text about people?

4 Allow the groups to work for about five minutes. Then stop the activity and ask how many questions each group has.
5 Ask the group with the largest number of questions to read them out. Ask the other groups to cross off questions that also appear on their lists.
6 Elicit any further questions from the rest of the class.
7 Tell the class to look for answers to the questions as they read the text.

## FALSE INFORMATION

**8.9**

**MATERIALS**
Copies of a rewritten paragraph from the text which includes false information

**LEVEL**
Intermediate +

**SKILLS**
Reading; Explaining; Skimming

**TIME**
10–15 minutes

**SUGGESTED TEXTS**
Articles on general knowledge

This activity is particularly useful for getting students to interact with texts on general knowledge. Students who already know the answers will glory in their knowledge, instantly spotting the false information. For the other students, the activity will simply be a guessing activity which will help them interact with the text.

### Preparation

Choose a paragraph from the text you are about to read. Rewrite it, keeping the original almost intact but including one or two sentences with false information. Make one copy for each student in the class.

### Procedure

1. Give out copies of the paragraph with false information to the students. Tell them that it is a paragraph taken from the text they are going to read, but that it contains a specified number of items of false information. Ask them to read it carefully and locate the two (or however many you choose to include) items of false information. Give them about two minutes to do this.
2. Divide the class into groups of three to five. In their groups, they discuss which information is false and why.
3. In plenary, listen to reports from the groups. In some groups a consensus will have been reached while in others there will be as many opinions as there are students.
4. Give out the complete text. Ask students to skim the text until they find the paragraph you have chosen and verify their answers.

## WHY DID IT HAPPEN?

**8.10**

**MATERIALS**
None

**LEVEL**
Intermediate +

**SKILLS**
Predicting; Expressing doubt

**TIME**
10–15 minutes

**SUGGESTED TEXTS**
Longer or shorter fiction

In life, as in fiction, influential events which alter our lives beyond recognition sometimes happen. Very often we feel helpless and out of control. Fiction writers recognise this universal predicament. It is this experience which *Why did it happen?* taps as students interact with a text.

### Preparation

Choose any three events which occur in the story you are going to read with your class. Write them on the board before the lesson starts. For example, you may write:

Frank decided to keep his name secret.
Eveline had to leave her home.
Mark lost all his money.

## Procedure

1 Divide the class into small groups.
2 Ask each group to appoint a secretary.
3 Tell them that the events written on the board happen in the story they are going to read. Ask each group to choose one event and brainstorm for at least ten possible reasons why it might have happened. The first group to finish may choose a second event.
4 It may be helpful to write expressions on the board such as:
*Maybe it happened because ...*
*Perhaps ...*
*It could be that ...*
*He/she might have ...*
*It's just possible that ...*
Tell the class to use these as they present their possibilities. The secretary should write down all the ideas presented.
5 In plenary, elicit all the suggestions. Ask students not to repeat suggestions already brought up.
6 Tell students to look for these events as they read the story.

**VARIATION**

For classes and teachers who enjoy competition, you could use the following variation.
1 Write only one event on the board.
2 When the students are in groups, ask each group to give itself a name.
3 Allow only three minutes for the collection of suggestions about 'why it might have happened'.
4 Write the name of each group of the board.
5 Each group contributes one idea at a time and is given a point for it. Any group that gives an idea which was previously presented loses a point.
6 The group with the most ideas wins.
Students whose voices are usually not heard in class should be nominated as spokespeople, but they may be advised in whispers by the others.

CHAPTER 9

# *Two heads are better than one*

## *Using pairing techniques*

As teachers we know that often we only learn and understand something thoroughly after we have explained it to someone else. That is why it seems quite natural that we should use pairwork a great deal in the EFL class. This chapter presents activities that involve a lot of work with a partner.

## PROVERBIALLY YOURS

**9.1**

**MATERIALS**
Proverbs written on slips of paper; Bag or hat

**LEVEL**
Intermediate +

**SKILLS**
Speaking; Listening

**TIME**
15–20 minutes

**SUGGESTED TEXTS**
Fiction, articles about values or other social issues

We often don't realise how frequently proverbs get used in everyday speech. Only after I started teaching them, did I begin to notice that a TV murder mystery described its bookish hero with the proverb, 'All work and no play makes Jack a dull boy', and that an American politician urged voters to give him support, because 'A new broom sweeps clean.'

Proverbs used to reflect cultural values and attitudes. However, in a world of rapidly changing social mores, proverbs are no longer thought of as truisms, but only descriptions of the way people thought the world ought to be. This activity both allows students to explore certain values in the culture of the target language, and permits them to share related aspects of their own culture.

### Preparation

1 Choose enough proverbs for half of the class. Make sure that at least one of them can somehow be related to the text you are later going to read. Some good proverbs are:

Rome wasn't built in a day
Out of sight out of mind
A bird in the hand is worth two in the bush
All that glitters is not gold
Where there is smoke there is fire
A penny saved is a penny earned

Experience is the best teacher
Do not count your chickens before they are hatched.
Charity begins at home
Look before you leap
Birds of a feather flock together

2 Write your chosen proverbs on slips of paper and cut these slips in half so the first half of each proverb is on one slip, and the second on another. Jumble the half-slips in a bag or hat.

## Procedure

1 Let each student pick a slip out of the hat.
2 Tell the students to walk around the room trying to locate their partner – the person who has the other half of their proverb. For less able classes, write out the entire proverbs on the board. When you see that most have found their partner, help the stragglers, so that everyone can settle down to work.
3 As soon as everyone has found their partner, ask them to sit together and allow them ten minutes to decide on the following:
- What does their proverb mean?
- Can they think of a specific example or story from life which might illustrate the proverb?
- Do they agree with the general truth expressed in the proverb? (If not, then why not?)
- Is there a comparable proverb in their native language?

4 Elicit answers from as many pairs as seems interesting, but don't drag this out. If you have not done so previously, write all the proverbs on the board as they are being discussed.
5 Tell the class the general content of the text you are about to read and ask if any of the proverbs discussed might have any connection with such a text. Accept all answers and explanations.

# DOUBLE VISION

## 9.2

**MATERIALS**
Natural scenery pictures (woods, lakes, farms, etc.)

**LEVEL**
Elementary +

**SKILLS**
Speaking; Listening; Asking questions

**TIME**
10–15 minutes

**SUGGESTED TEXTS**
Any text which deals with nature, nature preservation or ecology

*Double vision* involves the use of pictures and texts in a simple pairing activity. The activity helps students to review nature vocabulary and thus prepares them for any text connected with nature, natural phenomena, nature preservation or ecology.

## Preparation

Look for nature pictures such as postcards or pictures from travel magazines. If possible, mount them on cardboard. Cut each picture in half vertically.

## Procedure

1 Hand out a 'half picture' to each student. Tell them to hold it so that no one else can see it.
2 Their task now is to walk around the room finding the person who has the other part of their picture. While doing this they are not to show their picture to anyone. They must find out what pictures other students have by asking questions about that person's picture. They can ask such questions as:
Does your picture have a river in it?
Does your picture have a house with a red roof?
Only after students are almost certain that they are indeed talking to the person who has the other half of their picture can they look at each other's pictures. (In an elementary class, you should probably revise vocabulary and question-asking before asking them to locate their partners.)
3 As soon as everyone has found their partner, ask them to sit together and do the following:
   i Review all the vocabulary from the picture. They should ask other pairs in the room, or you, if any word is not known to them.
   ii Decide whether or not they like their picture and why they like or dislike it. They needn't agree on this.
4 Bring the whole class together. Look at and discuss a few of the pictures. Tell them the topic of the text they are going to read and ask them to brainstorm for possible connections between the picture and the text.

ACKNOWLEDGEMENT
I learned this activity from Tessa Woodward in 1986 when I took a summer course from her at Pilgrims at the University of Kent, Canterbury, England.

## 9.3

**MATERIALS**
Slips of paper; Bag or hat; Large sheets of drawing paper; Felt pens; A dictionary; sellotape or Blu-tack

**LEVEL**
Intermediate +

**SKILLS**
Speaking; Scanning; Writing

**TIME**
15–20 minutes

**SUGGESTED TEXTS**
Any text

# WORDS ON THE DOUBLE

This activity permits preteaching of much of the important vocabulary you want students to have for active use in the text they are going to read. As a fringe benefit, you also get a cheerful, nicely decorated classroom!

## Preparation

1. Go through the text you are planning to read and copy out the words or phrases you want to teach for active use on slips of paper.
2. Next to each word, write the number of the page and paragraph it came from. Write three words on each slip of paper.
3. Photocopy each slip of paper, so you have two copies of each.
4. Make as many slips as there are students in your class. If you have an uneven number of students, make three slips for one set of words. If you don't have enough words to give out three words to each pair, repeat some of the words. But remember that for each repetition there must also be an identical 'partner slip'.

   Put the sheets of paper, the felt pens, the dictionary and the sellotape or Blu-tack in a convenient place where they can be reached by everyone.

## Procedure

1. Ask the students to pull one slip each from the bag or hat.
2. Ask the students to walk around the room and find one person who has exactly the same words as them. If you have an uneven number of students, three students can find each other and form a threesome.
3. When they have paired up, partners check that at least one of them knows the words they have been assigned. If neither knows, they may look them up in a dictionary, ask other students or ask you to explain the meanings.
4. Once they know the meanings of their words, they look in the text and locate them according to the page and paragraph numbers on the slips. Once they find the sentence in which each word was used, they copy that sentence colourfully on a sheet of paper. Students who are able to do so may also wish to add their own, original, sentence using the new word, right under the sentence from the text. If they wish, students may decorate the 'word poster' they have made. They can then put it on the wall using sellotape or Blu-tack.
5. Once all the posters are up, each pair reads its own sentences and explains the words to the rest of the class.
6. Tell the class to be on the lookout for these words as they read the text.

## TWIN PARAGRAPHS

### 9.4

**MATERIALS**
Slips of paper; Bag or hat

**LEVEL**
Intermediate +

**SKILLS**
Skimming; Summarising

**TIME**
15–20 minutes

**SUGGESTED TEXTS**
Any articles or essays

*Twin paragraphs* is good prereading for a difficult text as it involves a great deal of skimming and pre-digestion of the text.

### Preparation

Go through the text and, on slips of paper, write the first and last lines of enough paragraphs to distribute slips to half of the students. Make duplicates for distribution to the other half of the class. If you have an uneven number of students in your class, make one set of three copies. If the whole reading passage has fewer paragraphs than half of the students in your class, make several copies of some lines.
Here is how a slip should look:

The first line of your paragraph is *Few people realise the danger they are in.*

The last line of your paragraph is *Perhaps that is the only solution.*

Put all the slips in the bag or hat.

### Procedure

1 Ask the students to take one slip each from the bag or hat.
2 Ask them to walk around the room looking for a partner who has exactly the same slip.
3 When they have found their partners, they sit together and skim through the text looking for their own paragraph.
4 When they have found their paragraph, they read it carefully, extracting the main ideas, and summarising it.
5 Bring the whole class together and listen to the paragraph summaries. This is especially interesting if two pairs have read the same paragraph. There may then be some disagreement and the whole class will be forced to look at this particular paragraph.

## 9.5

**MATERIALS**
Slips of paper; Bag or hat

**LEVEL**
Intermediate +

**SKILLS**
Skimming; Predicting

**TIME**
10–15 minutes

**SUGGESTED TEXTS**
Short stories, novels or plays

# MATCHING CHARACTERS

Introducing the cast of characters prior to reading about them is helpful both for motivation and comprehension. This activity gives students an opportunity to skim the text to gather as much information as possible about the people they will meet and to speculate imaginatively on the basis of that information.

## Preparation

1 Go through the text you are going to read making a list of the characters and the page numbers where they appear.
2 Write the name of one character and the page numbers where this character appears in the text on slips of paper. Write out enough slips for half of the class and make a copy of each of them. Repeat character names as many times as needed. For example, if I have twenty students in my class and there are four characters in the story, I would make ten slips of paper based on the four characters. This means that characters would have to be repeated, but page numbers need not be. If my characters are Martha, Susan, Peter and David my ten slips might look as follows:

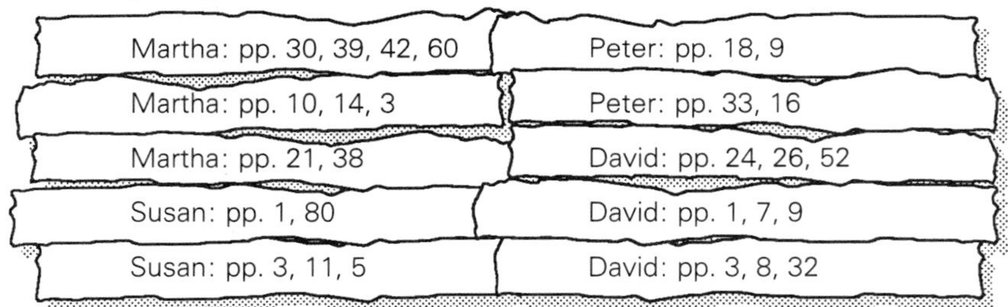


## Procedure

1 Put all the slips in a bag or hat and ask students to pick one each.
2 Ask the students to walk around the room and find the person who has the identical slip of paper. Warn them to check the page numbers as well as the names of characters.
3 Once students have found their partners, they should sit together and skim the pages on which their character appears, trying to find out as much information as possible about this character. They might also speculate about the importance of this character in the story, their physical appearance and relationship to other characters. The pairs should make notes on their conclusions as they will, later, have to report to the class.
4 Bring the whole class together and ask about the characters one at a time. Invite all the pairs to contribute. There will be discussion and much disagreement as students will have made different speculations about their characters, depending on which part of the text they read.
5 Tell students to be on the lookout for their characters as they read the text.

## LEND ME YOUR PEN

**9.6**

**MATERIALS**
None

**LEVEL**
Elementary +

**SKILLS**
Listening; Speaking

**TIME**
5–10 minutes

**SUGGESTED TEXTS**
Any factual text

Any general information text lends itself well to this activity. Students are sometimes surprised when they realise how much they already know about a certain topic. I have used this introduction to articles as diverse as an autobiographical essay by Helen Keller, an article about an escaped tiger and a passage on how coffee is grown.

### Procedure

1 Ask half of the students to give you their pens. Hold all these pens like a bouquet of flowers in your hand.
2 Ask the students who have not given you a pen (the other half of the class) to pick one of the pens you are holding. The person whose pen they have picked is their partner.
3 Ask the students to find their partners and sit together.
4 Tell them the subject of the article they are about to read and ask them to pool all the information they have on this subject. They should jot down all their ideas. While they do this, move among them, getting some pairs started and helping out with vocabulary.
5 Bring the whole group together and ask for bits of information. Summarise the material on the board.

## LEND ME YOUR EAR

**9.7**

**MATERIALS**
None

**LEVEL**
Intermediate +

**SKILLS**
Listening; Speaking

**TIME**
10–15 minutes

**SUGGESTED TEXTS**
Any text that can be related to students' own experience

This activity divides pairwork into two distinct tasks – that of listener and that of speaker. This is a good way of activating those reticent speakers who, even in small group or pair situations, tend to keep quiet while others dominate. The activity serves as a good introduction to any text that can be related to students' personal experience.

### Preparation

Read through the text you will be using and decide on a topic related to the text that also has some relevance to the lives of your students.

### Procedure

1 Tell the students that they are going to have two jobs. One will be as a speaker, the other as a listener. Make two columns on the board. One should be labelled 'Speaker', the other 'Listener'. Ask, 'What do speakers try to accomplish when they talk, either to a group or to an individual?' Listen to all responses and make a list on the board. Your list under speaker might look as follows:

Share information
Communicate
Be friendly
Show liking or approval
Be interesting

Then ask, 'How can listeners show that they are really paying attention to the speaker?' This time your list may look as follows:

Smiling
Head nodding
Seating position
Gestures
Not interrupting
Asking relevant questions

**2** Ask the students to sit in pairs facing each other. Tell them that for two minutes each of them is going to be a speaker while the other is a listener. The listener is not to interrupt, not to ask questions but to show they are attentively listening while the speaker speaks.
**3** Assign the letters A and B to the pairs. A will be the first speaker and B the first listener.
**4** Give them your chosen topic and allow a few seconds of thinking time. Signal for A students to start.
**5** Allow them three minutes. Give the signal to stop. Ask the speaker to tell their listener whether they felt that they had really been listened to and in what ways they were made aware of having the listener's full attention. Allow about half a minute for this.
**6** Signal for B speakers to begin and repeat the procedure.
**7** Tell them in what way the text they are about to read relates to what they have been speaking about.

ACKNOWLEDGEMENT
This activity is a variation of a technique I learned from Dr Ora Zohar at the Center for Teaching Improvement at the Hebrew University School of Education, Jerusalem, Israel.

# FILL ME IN

## 9.8

**MATERIALS**
Slips of paper; Bag or hat

**LEVEL**
Elementary +

**SKILLS**
Skimming; Predicting; Asking questions

**TIME**
10–15 minutes

**SUGGESTED TEXTS**
Any text

This activity pre-digests some of the information from the text to be read and gives it to the students. By looking at this students can speculate on the content of the complete text. This helps to arouse curiosity about the text and provides motivation for reading it.

## Preparation

1 Read through the text you plan to study and make a list of questions and answers about it. Write enough questions for half of the class and enough answers for the second half of the class on slips of paper. The answers must be very clear and unambiguous. If the text is long the answer slips should also have the page number where the answers can be found. Prepare one extra answer slip if you have an uneven number of students in your class.
2 Put all the question and answer slips into a bag or hat.

## Procedure

1 Ask each student to pull one slip from the bag or hat.
2 Tell them that their slip is either an answer or a question on the text they will be reading. Ask them to find their partner. The question slip student should be looking for the matching answer slip student and the answer slip student should be looking for the matching question.
3 Ask them to walk about the room and find each other.
4 As soon as everyone has found their partner, they should look at the text to find information that verifies their answer.
5 In plenary, ask the students to read out the questions, answers and all the information found in the text.
6 Ask the class to predict the content of whole text.

## 9.9

**MATERIALS**
None

**LEVEL**
Advanced

**SKILLS**
Speaking;
Explaining

**TIME**
15–20 minutes

**SUGGESTED TEXTS**
Essays or articles on controversial issues

# MAKE A CHOICE

*Make a choice* is a twist on an old values-clarification technique that I have seen used in a variety of ways. You have probably used it yourself. I have adapted this technique to pairwork and found it to be a fine introduction for any reading passage that deals with a controversial issue.

## Procedure

1. Draw two large chalk circles on the floor – one on each side of the room. Ask students to move their chairs if necessary. Tell students that the circle on the right-hand side of the room represents a warm climate while the circle on the left represents a cold climate. Ask all those who prefer living in a warm climate to go and stand in the right-hand circle while those who prefer living in a cold climate to go and stand in the left-hand circle.
2. When everyone is inside one of the circles, ask students to turn to the person next to them and explain why they prefer the climate they have chosen.
3. Ask the students to pair up with a person from the other circle and try to convert them to their own choice of climate. In classes where more students prefer one climate to another, some of these groups will have to form threesomes in which two students try to convince one and one tries to convince two. The lonely advocate may ask for help from another pair.
4. If time permits, repeat this procedure with summer/winter; theatre/cinema; ocean/lake; desert/wood or any other contrasting pair.
5. Bring the class together and tell them that there are always at least two sides to any issue.
6. Tell them about the controversial issue they are going to read about and try to elicit two ways of looking at the problem.

## ONLY CHILD

## 9.10

**MATERIALS**
None

**LEVEL**
Intermediate +

**SKILLS**
Explaining; Asking questions

**TIME**
10–15 minutes

**SUGGESTED TEXTS**
Any dealing with family relationships

This is a suitable introduction for any text dealing with family relationships, parents and children, sibling rivalry, etc. The activity allows for introspection and sharing, and fosters intimacy in the class.

### Procedure

1 Write the word *sibling* on the board and explain the meaning – brother or sister. Explain that among *siblings* you also include step-children or foster children. Ask your class how many of them had four or more siblings. Wait for hands to be raised. Ask how many had three siblings? How many had two? How many were only-children?
2 Ask students to form groups according to the number of siblings in their families. Four or more is considered a large family and they form one group.
3 Ask students to turn to the person next to them and talk about what it was like to be a member of large, small, or medium-sized families. Ask them to tell each other whether they were oldest, youngest or middle child in their families and if this had any effect on them.
4 Ask students to move about and find a person from a very different sized family. This time they might compare the advantages and disadvantages of being an only-child as opposed to having lots of brothers and sisters.
5 Bring the class back together and talk about qualities of people who come from large families. Do they know how to share better? Do they get along with people better? What about only-children? Are they closer to their parents? Are they less independent? What about middle children? Is it true that they are very competitive?
6 Tell them that they are about to read a text that deals with family issues.

## CHAPTER 10

# *Puzzling it out*

## *Using jigsaw techniques*

An interesting way of conceptualising the whole is to first encounter pieces of it and then fit the pieces together. The idea of the jigsaw puzzle as a learning technique was comprehensively presented by Elliot Aronson *et al* in his book *The Jigsaw Classroom* (Sage Publications 1978). Aspects of this technique are used here as pre-text activities.

To someone who has never used them, the jigsaw techniques at first appear bulky and cumbersome. However, once you try them and make them part and parcel of your teaching repertoire, you will love them and use them over and over again, simply because they are so communicative and generate such a great deal of student involvement. The extra bit of preparation in putting together these activities is really very simple and, in the long run, well worth the effort.

### 10.1 THE ROUNDABOUT

**MATERIALS**
Copies of sections of the text

**LEVEL**
Intermediate +

**SKILLS**
Reading; Summarising; Asking questions

**TIME**
15–20 minutes

**SUGGESTED TEXTS**
Longer prose selections

This is a reading activity which grows very lively. Students who have been given a passage from the middle of the text are often frustrated at first. They may vent their frustration by asking all sorts of rather aggressive questions. As these questions are answered by other students, frustration is replaced by satisfaction.

#### Preparation

Divide the text you are about to read into seven to ten sections. Photocopy enough sections so that everyone in the class has a piece of text to read. The number of duplications doesn't matter, as long as at least one person is reading each piece of text. If your class is weak or your text particularly difficult, you might have to provide a glossary with each reading section.

#### Procedure

1 Give a section of text to each member of the class. Some will be reading sections also read by others while some will be the sole reader of their section. Their task is to write three questions about things they don't understand in the text. For example, someone might write:

There is a person called Jane in my part. Who is she?
or Edna, in my part, is very much afraid. Why?
or Julian seems to hate his mother. Why?

While they do this, circulate helping out with vocabulary and question formation.

2 In plenary, students ask each other their questions. As they give answers, write them, but not the questions, on the board.
3 After all the questions have been asked and answers given, ask students to guess the content of the entire text. Since each student has only read only one section this should generate a lot of guesswork.
4 Ask the students who have read the first and last sections of the text to talk about (not read out loud) their sections.
5 Ask the class if this adds anything to their speculations about the text.

## ORDER! ORDER!

**10.2**

**MATERIALS**
Copies of a summary of the text

**LEVEL**
Elementary +

**SKILLS**
Reading; Summarising

**TIME**
15–20 minutes

**SUGGESTED TEXTS**
Any longer text

I find this activity most useful as a preview of a longer extensive reading. For example, before we begin reading a novel which the students will be reading on their own at home, we do this activity and then read Chapter One together in class. However, teachers of elementary classes have told me that they have happily used the technique as a guided prereading to many shorter intensive reading texts.

### Preparation

If you are going to use a longer extensive text, prepare a five-paragraph summary of it. For example, on page 106 is a five-paragraph summary of Charles Dickens' *Great Expectations*. If you are going to use a short text, divide the whole text into five sections. Label the sections randomly A, B, C, D, and E, as in the sample text.

### Procedure

1 Divide the class into groups of five.
2 Give each group a complete set of five sections. Each student in the group reads their own section and makes sure they understand it. While they are reading, circulate helping out with vocabulary.
3 As soon as the individual reading is finished, students tell each other the content of the section each one has read.
4 The task of each group is to put the sections in the correct order and to give the entire passage a title.
5 The first group to finish stands in front of the class and tells (not *reads* but *tells*) the content of their passage.
6 Other groups add to and/or correct the information.

**E** The story we are going to read starts in the English countryside about one hundred years ago. We meet a small orphan boy, Pip, whom we find at the cemetery next to the gravestones of his parents. There, he meets an escaped convict for whom he later steals some food and a file. The convict is caught by the police and put back in prison. Pip is invited by a rich old woman, Miss Havisham, to come and play at her mansion. There he meets and falls in love with Estella, Miss Havisham's adopted daughter. Estella is very proud. She humiliates Pip and makes him feel that she can never possibly love him because he is so common. More than anything else, Pip wants to become a 'gentleman' for Estella's sake, but he has not the slightest hope of this, as it is planned that he is to become a blacksmith in the village.

**B** Then one day, out of the blue, Pip is visited by a lawyer from London, Mr Jaggers, who tells him that he has 'great expectations'. Some mysterious person, whose identity Pip must not know, has decided to invest a great deal of money in turning Pip into a 'gentleman'. Pip is told to go to London where he is to be given a generous allowance every month. He must simply learn how to eat, talk, walk and behave as if he had been born wealthy. He will even be placed in lodgings together with another young man who is a real gentleman just so that he can learn good manners.

**A** Pip happily goes to London, not glancing backward once. He quickly forgets all his old friends in the village. This is especially sad for Joe, the blacksmith, Pip's brother-in-law, who had been like a second father to the boy. But Pip cannot think about such things. He is dazzled with his new life and with his hopes of becoming enough of a gentleman to marry Estella. He is absolutely certain that the mysterious stranger who is providing the money for his education is none other than Miss Havisham who, he is sure, must want him to marry Estella.

**D** One rainy night a strange, uncouth, wet and wild-looking old man appears in Pip's lodgings. Pip is, at first, badly frightened. But as he and the wild man talk, Pip realises that this is the convict whom he had helped when he was a little child. Furthermore, Pip soon learns that this is the man who has provided for his education. The convict, as it turns out, had been shipped off to Australia, where he became a wealthy sheep farmer. He never forgot the kindness of the little boy and decided that Pip should have all his money.

**C** Now many things happen fast. Pip is at first shocked by his crude benefactor. Then, he suddenly grows up and realises many things. For the first time he recognises what a snob he has become. He realises that money does not 'make the man' and he begins to have real feelings of affection for the convict. The convict, however, is not allowed to be in England and can at any time be caught by the authorities. Pip must try to help him escape. This proves, at first, to be very difficult and later to be impossible.

Does Pip ever marry Estella? Ah, to answer that question, you will have to read the book.

## CLASSIC JIGSAW

**10.3**

**MATERIALS**
Copies of sections of the text

**LEVEL**
Intermediate +

**SKILLS**
Reading; Summarising; Explaining

**TIME**
30–40 minutes

**SUGGESTED TEXTS**
Any non-fiction text

This is a communicative reading technique which promotes group cooperation and allows participation by weaker students who are nicely manipulated into the position of experts. As a prereading technique, *Classic jigsaw* provides useful summarising and predicting elements.

### Preparation

1. Divide each text into four sections and make a copy of each section for every member of the class.
2. Label the four sections A, B, C and D, following the order of the content.
3. Put all the As in one pile, all the Bs in another pile, and so on.
4. Number the As consecutively A1, A2, A3, A4 – A1, A2, A3, A4 . . . until you run out of As. Follow the same procedure for the Bs, Cs and Ds.

### Procedure

1. Give out the reading sections. Each student will get only one reading section, an A, a B a C or a D. Hand the reading sections out in such a way that most As sit close to each other, Bs close to each other and so on.
2. Ask the students to silently read their section, make notes of the important ideas in it and summarise it. While they do this, circulate among them, helping out with vocabulary.
3. Ask the students to find other people who have read the same section and sit together in groups. You will now have four groups – one of As, one of Bs, one of Cs and one of Ds. If your class is large, you can simply split each group in two and have two groups of As, two groups of Bs, etc.
   The task of these groups is to discuss the contents of their passage and reach an agreement on its most important elements. They write a group summary which each group member copies and keeps. Stress to them that no one is to leave this group until they can present and teach the material that the group has read, since in the next stage each student will become an expert on the material of this section.
4. Ask students to sit together with those who have the same number (1, 2, 3, or 4) written on their slips. This will automatically give you groups containing an A, B, C, and D. If the groups are too large, you can again split them, but each group must have at least one A, one B, one C and one D. It doesn't matter if one group winds up with two Bs or Cs – this simply means two experts.
   The task of these groups is to teach each other the content of their sections. A goes first, B goes next, etc.
5. If you have time, bring the whole group together and briefly discuss the content of the entire text.

## 10.4

**MATERIALS**
Four pictures or 'word pictures' showing significant scenes from the story

**LEVEL**
Elementary +

**SKILLS**
Describing; Explaining

**TIME**
15–20 minutes

**SUGGESTED TEXTS**
Any fiction

# PICTURE JIGSAW

This activity involves visualisation or the use of real pictures with the additional challenge of putting a puzzle together. The whole idea revolves around four pictures which together give a good clue of what the story, novel or play you are going to read will be about.

## Preparation

Prepare four pictures (in very large classes duplicate each picture so that you have eight instead of four) which depict scenes from the story. Either draw them yourself, or ask a talented student to draw them, or use 'word pictures'. (See Note below)

## Procedure

1. Divide the class into four groups (eight groups in very large classes). This activity works better if the students stand up. Since this must be a strictly oral activity, students are less tempted to write from a standing position.
2. Give each group a picture. They should not show their picture to anyone outside their group. Their task is to study the picture carefully so that they will be able to remember it and describe it to someone who has not seen it. If you have given them a word picture, they should add details to it, such as the colour of people's clothes, the weather, the mood of the people in the picture, and anything else they might wish to add. No one should write anything down.
3. Take away the pictures.
4. Ask the students to form new groups in which there is at least one representative of each earlier group.
5. Ask the students to tell each other about their pictures.
6. Bring the whole class together and ask each group to talk about their picture. Allow comments and variations. Write a brief summary of what you hear on board. (Do not show the pictures again!)
7. Ask students to predict the content of the text from the content of the pictures.

**NOTE**

If you have no artists handy, use 'word pictures', which are written descriptions of situations, each one on a separate piece of paper. For example, four word pictures based on *Cinderella* might be:

Picture 1 We see a wedding of a middle-aged man and woman. Three young girls are witnessing the ceremony. One of them is extremely pretty.

Picture 2 We see a pretty young girl washing a floor. She is crying. A middle-aged woman is standing above her scolding.

Picture 3 We see an elegant ball. Everyone is dancing. All eyes are on a lovely young couple in the centre.

Picture 4 We see a prince placing a crown on the head of a beautiful princess.

## HALF A LOAF

## 10.5

**MATERIALS**
Copies of halves of text; A pair of scissors

**LEVEL**
Intermediate +

**SKILLS**
Scanning; Predicting; Asking questions

**TIME**
15–20 minutes

**SUGGESTED TEXTS**
Short articles or essays

This is the kind of activity which will encourage scanning and reading without the knowledge of every word. Students quickly become aware of the fact that they can understand a great deal of a text even if they only have one half of it.

### Preparation

Photocopy enough copies of the complete text for half of the students in your class.

### Procedure

1 Show the class a copy of the text they are going to read and then, in front of them, cut the text vertically down the middle. (This is a nice piece of drama. There is always some shouting of *No* and a few angry hisses!)
2 Tell them this unkind cut was deliberate and meant to show them how much sense one can make from a text even when one only reads half of it.
3 Give each student half of the text. Give one side of the room one half, the other side the other half.
4 Ask every student to read their own piece of text and jot down what they think are the main ideas in it.
5 Ask the students to sit in pairs. Each partner should have read a different half. They tell each other what they have understood from their half of the text, and ask each other questions about the other half.
6 Bring the whole group together. Ask them what they have understood about the contents of the text and write a short summary on the board.

**VARIATION**
When using longer texts, use only the first paragraph of the complete text for halving and from it predict the contents of the complete text.

## 10.6

**MATERIALS**
Slips of paper or index cards

**LEVEL**
Elementary +

**SKILLS**
Listening; Predicting

**TIME**
5–10 minutes

**SUGGESTED TEXTS**
Any text

# LISTENING JIGSAW

*Listening jigsaw* is a quick way into the text. It integrates listening and reading skills and is an easy activity to prepare. As listening material, you can use small sections of the complete text to be read or you can use a short anecdote which in some ways relates to the text.

## Preparation

Choose six short sections from the text you are going to be reading with the class and write each section (about four or five lines of text) clearly on an index card or slip of paper. Do not number or label the cards.

## Procedure

1. Hand out the six cards to different students sitting anywhere in the class. Do not give cards to students sitting close together. Try giving cards to good readers. Let these students have a few seconds to study the cards.
2. While these students are looking over their cards, tell the rest of the class that they will soon hear some pieces of text read out loud and it will be their job to arrange these pieces in the correct order.
3. Ask the students who have been given cards to read their material out loud. Call on readers in random order.
4. Ask the readers to repeat their readings in a different order.
5. Ask the class if they want any section of the reading repeated.
6. Ask the readers to come to the front of the room and stand in any order they wish.
7. Ask a volunteer in the class to come and arrange them in what they think is the correct order.
8. If need be, call on several students to have a try at this.
9. Read the passage in the correct order to the students. Tell them that what they have just heard is part of the text they will read and that they should look out for it as they progress in their reading of the text, or, if you have used an anecdote, tell them why that story is related to the text they will read.

# MESSENGER JIGSAW

## 10.7

**MATERIALS**
Copies of paragraphs taken from the text

**LEVEL**
Intermediate +

**SKILLS**
Reading; Listening; Predicting

**TIME**
20–25 minutes

**SUGGESTED TEXTS**
Any text

*Messenger Jigsaw* combines dictation with puzzle-solving activities. The activity stimulates competition among the groups as well as a lot of helpful cooperation within the group.

There will always be one or two students in the group who instantly grasp the dictated message. They can help others who struggle as the messenger dashes out for new information. If the group wants to swap messengers in mid-activity, because they find their original messenger too slow, by all means let them.

## Preparation

1 Choose four short paragraphs from the text, label them A to D and photocopy them. If the class is very large, make two copies of each paragraph so that you have eight pieces of text.
2 Stick these pieces of text on the wall outside your classroom. Stick as many pieces of text as there will be small groups in your class.

## Procedure

1 Divide the class into small groups of about five students.
2 Appoint one 'messenger' per group.
3 The job of the messenger is to go out of the room, choose one of the texts on the wall, memorise as much of it as possible, dash back to the class and dictate it to the rest of their group. (Each messenger should pick a different piece of text.) The messengers should try to be as quick and accurate as possible. They can go out to read the text as many times as they like.

   The group that writes the whole paragraph first wins and gets to read its paragraph. This is, however, only a temporary victory, as the paragraph also has to be checked for accuracy.
4 As each group finishes its dictation, the messenger brings in the posted paragraph and the group checks their version for accuracy. The group to finish first with fewest mistakes is the real winner.
5 Tell the students that the paragraphs are from the text they are going to read. Ask a student from each group to read their paragraph out and, with the whole group, predict the contents of the entire text.

ACKNOWLEDGEMENT
This activity is based on *The Messenger and the Scribe*, an activity in the book *Dictation Many Ways* by Paul Davis and Mario Rinvolucri (CUP, 1988).

## 10.8

**MATERIALS**
A drawing of a geometric pattern

**LEVEL**
Intermediate +

**SKILLS**
Explaining;
Listening

**TIME**
10–15 minutes

**SUGGESTED TEXTS**
Any article on a controversial issue

# POINT OF VIEW

*Point of view* uses a simple drawing to show different perspectives on one issue. This is particularly suitable for a text on a controversial issue.

## Preparation

Prepare a drawing of a pattern or geometric shape, like the one below.

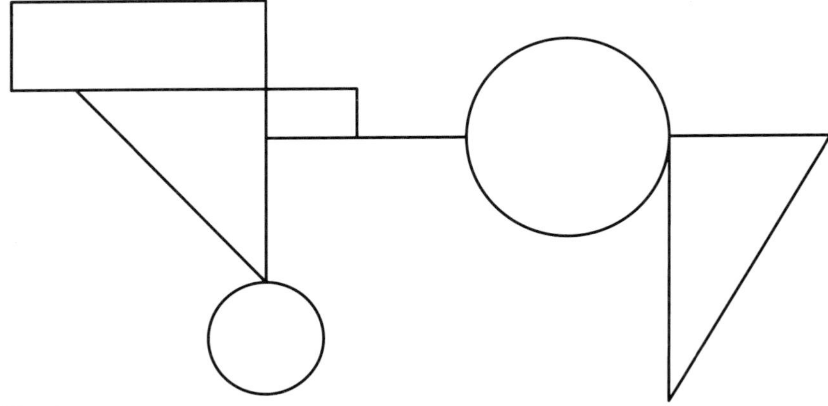

Fig. 6

## Procedure

1 Divide the class into small groups.
2 Ask each group to choose a representative.
3 Call the representatives to the front of the class and show them the geometric drawing. Their job is to return to their groups and explain how to draw it. The representatives are not allowed to demonstrate by drawing, but they may orally correct the students who are drawing. They may say, for example, 'Peggy, your lower triangle is too large'. They may encourage by saying 'Good!' The representatives may return as many times as they wish to look at the original drawing.
5 Stop this activity after about five minutes and ask all the students to hold up their drawings so that the whole class can see them. The drawings will invariably be different.
6 Write 'Point of view' on the board. Elicit the meaning of this phrase from the class. Relate the idea of points of view to controversial issues. Tell them the subject of the article that you are going to read. Ask them what some points of view on this issue might be.

## VOCABULARY CLUSTERS

This activity makes a puzzle of words for jigsaw prediction.

### Preparation

Read through the text you are going to teach, writing down the vocabulary items you want to teach for active use. Keep the words in the same order in which they appear in the text. Write four or five of these words on an index card. Make enough cards for each small group to have one.

### Procedure

1 Divide the class into small groups.
2 Give each group a vocabulary card.
3 Ask them to explain their words to each other. If no one in the group knows a word, they may ask you, or students in other groups or they may look up the word in a dictionary. Ask them to write sentences using the words. They may write one sentence for each word, or several words in one sentence. While they do this, write the words from all the cards on the board.
4 Ask each group to choose its best sentence and write it on the board. There will be lots of students up at the board writing at the same time.
5 Ask several students to read all the sentences on the board out loud.
6 Elicit or explain the meanings of all the words you have written on the board.
7 Tell the students that they have been working with vocabulary from the text they are going to read and ask them to predict the contents of the text. Tell them to look for the sentences in the text where 'their' words are used.

## 10.9

**MATERIALS**
Index cards; A dictionary

**LEVEL**
Beginner +

**SKILLS**
Vocabulary learning; Explaining; Listening; Predicting

**TIME**
20–25 minutes

**SUGGESTED TEXTS**
Any text

## 10.10

**MATERIALS**
Index cards

**LEVEL**
Advanced

**SKILLS**
Discussion;
Predicting;
Listening

**TIME**
15–20 minutes

**SUGGESTED TEXTS**
Longer works of fiction which will be read extensively

# GETTING TO KNOW YOU

This is a good introduction to a fiction text that has several important characters, especially a longer text which is to be read extensively.

The activity leans heavily on the evocative nature of names. Very frequently we develop a whole image of a person from just hearing their name.

## Preparation

Prepare one 'central character' card for each small group in the class. These cards should each have the name and description of one character from the text – the central character of that card – as well as a list of the names of all the characters which appear on the other character cards.
For example:

*Central character: Dora*

*She is a delicate young woman who is loved and protected by her father. She has a little dog called Jip. She marries early and becomes a very inadequate housekeeper. She dies young leaving a sorrowful husband.*

*Other characters: David*
*Aunt Betsy*
*Agnes*
*Little Emily*

*How do you think Dora is related to these other people?*

Fig. 7

Other groups will get cards with descriptions of other characters. Make sure that you don't give away the relationships between the characters in your descriptions.

## Procedure

1 Divide the class into small groups and ask each group to appoint a secretary.
2 Give each group a central character card.
3 Ask the groups to read the description of their central character and then to guess how the other characters listed on their cards might be related to that character. They should create an imagined description, similar to the one they were given for the central character, for

each of the other names. The secretary should write down all suggestions. Allow about five minutes for this activity.

**4** Call out the name of one central character, such as 'Dora'. Listen to all the speculations about this character from groups that did not have her as their central character. Let the group that received her as a central character speak last. Write her name on the board and continue to the next character.

**5** When all the characters are listed on the board, elicit guesses about their relationships. For example, a student might say, 'Dora must be David's wife, because the group which had David as a central character said that David's first wife died young and on our card it said that Dora married early and died young'.

**6** Tell the class that they will eventually meet all the people they have been talking about in the book they are about to read and that it will be interesting to check their assumptions.

## Bibliography

Aronson, E *et al* 1978 *The Jigsaw Classroom* Sage Publications
Azra, E and Hess, N 1988 *It Stands to Reason* Eric Cohen Books
Bartlett, J 1980 *Familiar Quotations* Little Brown and Co.
Davis, P and Rinvolucri, M 1988 *Dictation Many Ways* CUP
Frost, R 1979 *The Poetry of Robert Frost* Holt Rinehart and Winston
Johnson, T H 1960 *The Complete Poems of Emily Dickinson* Little Brown and Co.
Joyce, J 1967 *The Dubliners* Jonathan Cape
Oller, J and Richard-Amato, P (Eds) 1983 *Methods that Work* Newbury House
Peterson, R 1962 *Poetry II* Crowell-Collier Publishing Co.
Stevick, E 1980 *Teaching Languages: A Way and Ways* Newbury House
Ur, P 1981 *Discussions that Work: Task-centred Fluency Practice CUP*

## Further reading

Moskowitz, G 1978 *Caring and Sharing in the Foreign Language Classroom: A sourcebook on Humanistic Techniques* Newbury House

Nuttall, C 1987 *Teaching Reading Skills in a Foreign Language* Heinemann Educational Books

Rogers, C 1982 *Freedom to Learn for the Eighties* Charles E Merrill Publishing Co.

# Index

## Activities classified by type of text

**Fiction – shorter**

1.1 Line finding
1.4 Comparing quotations
1.6 Debatable quotations
1.7 Placing it
1.10 Close the gap
2.1 The mental video
2.2 Gates
2.7 The surrealistic picture
2.8 Making connections
2.9 Picture a symbol
3.1 The surprise package
3.3 Meaningful object
3.4 Kim's game
4.1 This makes me think of that
5.8 Letter of recommendation
7.2 Scrambled guessing
7.4 Best choice
7.6 Who is who?
7.7 Upside down who is who?
7.8 Divide and conquer
8.1 Gut reactions
8.2 Why, where and how?
8.3 Why do they do it?
8.5 Neighbours
8.7 A word of advice
8.10 Why did it happen?
9.5 Matching characters
10.4 Picture jigsaw

**Narratives**

1.7 Placing it
2.3 I'm in the picture

**Newspapers or magazines**

1.2 Treasure hunt
1.3 Needle in a haystack
7.1 It sits where it fits
7.3 Call it by name

**Non-fiction**

1.1 Line finding
2.8 Making connections
3.3 Meaningful object
3.4 Kim's game
10.3 Classic jigsaw

**Poems**

1.6 Debatable quotation
3.1 The surprise package
4.1 This makes me think of that
6.6 On your own
6.8 Pieces in place

**Songs**

6.8 Pieces in place
6.9 Filling spaces

**Plays**

9.5 Matching characters

**Technical texts**

3.7 Appliances
5.5 Mini lecture

# Index

## Activities classified by topic